Universities at the Crossroads

Universities at the Crossroads

ANDRÉ BÉTEILLE

OXFORD
UNIVERSITY PRESS

Oxford University Press is a department of the University of Oxford. It furthers the University's objective of excellence in research, scholarship, and education by publishing worldwide. Oxford is a registered trademark of Oxford University Press in the UK and in certain other countries

Published in India by
Oxford University Press
YMCA Library Building, 1 Jai Singh Road, New Delhi 110 001, India

First Edition published in 2010
Oxford India Paperbacks 2015

ISBN-13: 978-0-19-945525-6
ISBN-10: 0-19-945525-2

Typeset in Adobe Garamond Pro 11/12.73
at Digital Domain IT Services Pvt. Ltd., Kolkata
Printed in India at Replika Press Pvt. Ltd.

Dedicated to the memory of
Edward Shils
(1910–1995)

Contents

Acknowledgements

I have incurred many debts in the preparation of this volume. Several of the chapters included in it have been published before. Some (Chapters 1, 3, 10, and 12) have been printed but not published. Chapters 7 and 9 have been neither printed nor published before.

Chapters 1, 3, 10, and 12 were delivered as convocation addresses at the University of Calcutta (2006), at Rabindra Bharati University (2007), at the Tata Institute of Social Sciences (2001), and at the West Bengal National University of Juridical Sciences (2010), respectively. I am grateful to the authorities of the institutions mentioned for inviting me to play a part in their convocations. Chapter 2—'Universities as Public Institutions'—was delivered as the G. Ram Reddy Memorial Lecture at Hyderabad (2005), and Chapter 6—'Access to Education'—as the Kamala Lecture at the University of Calcutta (2008). They were both published in the *Economic and Political Weekly*, the former in vol. XL, no. 31, pp. 3377–81 (30 July 2005) and the latter in vol. XLIII, no. 20, pp. 148–56 (17 May 2008), and I am grateful to the editor for permission to reproduce them here. Chapter 4, 'Universities at the Crossroads', and Chapter 8, 'Institutions and Networks', were previously published in *Current Science*, the former in vol. 92, no. 4, pp. 441–9 (25 February 2007) and the latter in vol. 97, no. 2, pp. 148–56 (25 July 2009). I would like to thank the editor for permission to reproduce them here. Chapter 5—'The School and the Community'—was published in the *Journal of Educational Planning and Administration*, vol. XXI, no. 3, pp. 191–201 (July 2007), and Chapter 11—'Universities in the Twenty-first Century'—is being published in the same journal, vol. XXIII, no. 4, pp. 331–46 (October 2009). I am grateful to the editor of the journal for consenting to their publication here as well.

Chapter 9—'Social Science Research'—is based on a lecture delivered at the Indian Statistical Institute on 17 August 2007 on the occasion of its platinum jubilee. I am grateful to the authorities of the Institute, where I held my first research position, for inviting me to give the lecture which enabled me to draw upon some of my experience as chairman of the Indian Council of Social Science Research, a position I held at that time. Chapter 7—'The Making of an Inclusive Society'—is based on a lecture organized jointly by the New India Foundation and *The Telegraph* in Kolkata on 6 March 2009.

I would like to mention two persons in particular for their help and encouragement. When I asked Rudrangshu Mukherji what I should do with the lecture he had organized in Kolkata on behalf of *The Telegraph*, he suggested that I should put together the three or four lectures on similar subjects that he had heard, and publish them as a book; the two or three turned into a dozen and he very kindly read all of them. I would like also to thank Gopalkrishna Gandhi who sat through several of the lectures included here and urged me in particular to include the lecture on Social Science Research, which he had heard and which I had not included until he urged me to do so. He often acted as my host in Kolkata and always made me feel at home in Raj Bhavan, which was his residence for five years. This book will always remind me of the Wellesley suite where I spent many happy days and nights in his company and under his care.

—André Béteille

30 June 2010

Introduction

The essays and addresses brought together in this volume deal with the fortunes—and misfortunes—of the universities in our time. It does not include all that I have written on the universities. An earlier collection (Béteille 2000a) included three papers on the subject, dealing successively with the academic career, the university as a centre of learning, and the university as an institution. All the pieces in this collection were written subsequently to the publication of that volume.

I have published other articles and essays besides the aforementioned, both in newspapers such as *The Times of India*, *The Hindu*, and *The Telegraph*, and in scholarly periodicals such as *Minerva*. Most of the newspaper articles may be found in two volumes entitled *Chronicles of Our Time* (Béteille 2000b) and *Ideology and Social Science* (Béteille 2005).

My first sustained effort to examine the working of universities was the Duhr Memorial Lecture delivered at St Xavier's College, Bombay, in 1980, and published in *Minerva* as 'The Indian University: Academic Standards and the Pursuit of Equality' (Béteille 1981). My central interest as a sociologist has been in the study of inequality, its various forms and aspects, and the relations between its different dimensions. Until then, my main focus of interest had been on the changing relations between caste and class. The Duhr lecture kindled my interest in examining the limits to which the principle of equality can be realized in the practices of public institutions.

By the late 1970s, I was coming to appreciate the profound significance of the deep disjunction in all modern societies between the adoption of the ideal of equality and the obdurate reality of inequality in every social sphere. This disjunction, though present in every modern society, appeared to be particularly marked and acute in contemporary India. Public-spirited Indians are tireless in their advocacy of equality, and yet their own actions contribute in myriad ways to the perpetuation of inequality.

It is in this specific context that I began my sociological enquiry and analysis of the university. The study of the university has been for me a part of my more general interest in the interplay between the ideal of equality and the practice of inequality. Planners, policymakers, and public intellectuals, including those within the universities, have generally taken it for granted that the universities, if they undertake their tasks sincerely and resolutely, can contribute significantly to the creation of equality in a hierarchical society. This perception has gathered increasing strength in the 60 odd years since independence. It has been the main justification for the creation of new universities and the expansion of existing ones. The multiplication and expansion of universities has had unintended consequences since the academic objectives of the university have not been easy to harmonize with the social and political tasks assigned to it. I have tried to examine as a sociologist the unintended consequences of the rapid, not to say reckless, expansion of universities where it is driven by social and political, rather than academic, objectives.

The universities have played some part in challenging and disturbing existing social hierarchies. But beyond that the part that they can play in creating social equality is limited. The policy to use universities for creating social equality without consideration of the limits to which this can be done is misconceived, and sooner or later it comes to grief. The single-minded pursuit of such a policy leads to a diversion from the pursuit of science and scholarship, which is the primary objective of the university as a centre of learning and a social institution, into other channels.

When they were first set up in India in 1857, the universities created new opportunities for upward social mobility and a new horizon of possibilities for at least a certain section of the population. They initiated a process of churning whose social and cultural significance cannot be gainsaid. This was the burden of my address at the sesquicentennial convocation of the University of Calcutta, published as Chapter 1 of the present collection. The universities brought something new into the country, both as centres of learning and as social institutions.

Yet, the part they played in the process of social churning should not be exaggerated. In the nineteenth century, and well into the twentieth, the universities had only a limited reach across the population of the subcontinent. They and their colleges became the preserves of the middle class, which itself comprised a miniscule minority of the population. Beyond them lay the vast masses of peasants, artisans, and other manual workers whose awareness of university education was at best limited. The idea of a university education for all would appear strange in the nineteenth century even in the advanced Western countries. It was only after World War II and decolonization that such an idea began to gather support.

* * *

University expansion began in India in the wake of independence. It began at a time when universities were expanding everywhere, including the United States. The conditions under which higher education began to grow and spread differed from one country to another, but its expansion in the Western countries had a demonstration effect on less developed countries such as India. In the United States, those who looked back to the universities as they were before the War, noted the rise of what they called the 'mass university' in the second half of the twentieth century. Mass universities have become a common feature of the system of higher education in India. The University of Bombay, the University of Calcutta, and the University of Delhi are now very different in size and scale from what they were in the early decades of their existence.

I have in my own lifetime observed and experienced major changes in the structure and functioning of the Indian university. The University of Delhi is now a very different place from what it was when I entered its service in 1959. At the same time, it will be a mistake to think that the Indian university remained unchanged from the time of its first foundation until the time of independence. The University of Calcutta was a very different place in the nineteenth century from what it became under Sir Ashutosh Mukherji, who was its vice-chancellor between 1906 and 1914. Before his time, there was hardly any research done in the university, and teaching was undertaken not in the university but in the colleges affiliated with it.

The awareness of the continuing changes taking place in our universities—and in universities throughout the world—obliges us to take a historical view of the university as both a centre of learning and a social institution. Most of the universities that now exist in India, including the majority of central universities such as the Jawaharlal Nehru University, the North-Eastern Hill University, and the University of Hyderabad, have come up in my own lifetime, and indeed while I was already a university teacher. Someone who has witnessed and experienced so many changes in the recent past cannot help asking what the future holds for the university.

Our universities have grown so much in size that many now count their members in the hundreds of thousands. The size and scale of their operation make it difficult for them to function meaningfully as communities of scientists and scholars, which is, however, what many still think the universities should be. Nor is the principle of the unity of teaching and research easy to sustain in most of our universities today. As for the principle of self-governance, only its rituals rather than its substance may be observed in the majority of cases.

The pressures and compulsions under which university expansion has escalated in the last several decades come from both within and outside, and I have described and analysed them in the chapters of this volume. I have focused mainly on two kinds of pressures which may be called academic, and social or political. Academic pressures arise from the growth and differentiation of knowledge and the need to accommodate new disciplines and branches of knowledge; the accommodation of new subjects does not lead to the elimination of old ones although it does tend to lead to their neglect. Socio-political pressures arise from the need to accommodate disadvantaged classes and communities in increasing numbers and proportions.

The new colleges and universities are now producing large numbers of graduates and doctorates, but they have failed to satisfy the ever-growing hunger for university degrees. Their overall contribution to the creation of equality in society as a whole has been limited. The relationship between higher education and equality is uncertain and unpredictable, a fact that even those involved in educational planning and administration tend to ignore and overlook. It is simply not true that opening more universities and producing more graduates will automatically ensure greater equality overall. On the other hand, the overproduction of PhDs with little preparation or aptitude for research is likely to lead to the creation of what may be described as 'trained incapacity'.

While universities create opportunities for individual mobility which is in some sense a gain for equality, they also contribute to the reproduction of inequality. In an open system, success in academic competition depends only in part on individual merit and ability; it depends also, and sometimes very greatly, on the possession of material, cultural, and social capital. Social and cultural capital, not to speak of material capital, is very unevenly distributed in our society, its distribution being governed by family, class, and community. In any competition between two persons with roughly the same ability or talent, the one with the superior endowment of capital is likely to win unless the other person is favoured by luck. This is what leads to the reproduction of inequality. Individual mobility happens when persons who are poorly endowed materially and otherwise have unusual ability or unusual luck.

As I have pointed out at several places in the book, the Indian universities were from the beginning open and secular institutions. But they did not seek actively to be socially inclusive in the sense of striving deliberately to incorporate all classes and communities when they were first established. By today's standards they were in their early phase 'elitist', as indeed universities were throughout the world in the nineteenth century and well into the twentieth. They provided some opportunities for individual mobility, but by and large they did not interfere with the social reproduction of inequality. As a result, although admissions and appointments were in principle open to members of all classes and communities, both teachers and students came very largely from the upper castes and the middle classes.

The uneven distribution of castes and communities had become a source of worry even during colonial rule. Community-based quotas began to be introduced, mainly in peninsular India, and were already in place when the country became independent and then embarked on a course of university reform and expansion. A major impetus for expansion and reform came after 1977, and the demand gathered strength to make the universities socially more inclusive not only in principle but also in practice. Our record of using the universities to create a more inclusive society is discussed at several places, and particularly in Chapter 7.

In India, the policies and practices of the government have had a large influence on the universities. From the very beginning, it is the state rather than any religious establishment or private capital that has taken the initiative in establishing and maintaining the universities. Anyone who reflects and writes on the university, its past, present, and future, cannot avoid reviewing and commenting on matters of policy. The first universities in India were established by the colonial government which maintained a watch over not only their funding but also their functioning. Today, in independent India, the government can still make or mar the universities, although, unlike its predecessor, it never tires of expressing its solicitude for academic autonomy.

* * *

I have in these essays entered more closely and more directly into matters of policy than in my previous writings, except for my newspapers articles. The relationship between social theory and social policy is a complex one on which I have touched briefly in Chapter 10 which was, in fact, written before all the other ones.

Throughout my teaching in the Delhi School of Economics, which began in 1959, I have sought to articulate the distinction between value judgements and judgements of reality, and between social policy and social theory. In this I was greatly influenced by M.N. Srinivas with whom I was closely associated in the early part of my career. At that time, the influence of the Oxford anthropologists was very marked in Srinivas's thinking, and they, and in particular A.R. Radcliffe-Brown, regarded that distinction to be fundamental. When I first knew him, Srinivas had achieved great renown for his book on Coorg religion (Srinivas 1952) which was a descriptive and analytical study of an important aspect of Indian society that steered clear of questions of policy.

My own first book, *Caste, Class and Power* (Béteille 1965), was, again, primarily an exercise in the sociological analysis of an empirical problem. Unlike Srinivas's monograph, it had to deal with some of the consequences of major policy decisions, such as those relating to agrarian reform and local self-government, but I was determined to deal with them empirically and not normatively. In this I was strongly encouraged by M.N. Srinivas who often pointed out that, at least in India, sociologists who yielded to the temptation of proffering advice on policy rarely succeeded in avoiding platitudes. Although I was already familiar with some of Max Weber's basic ideas, it was only later that I encountered his argument that, unlike the 'dogmatic disciplines' such as jurisprudence, logic, ethics, and aesthetics, sociology and history are 'empirical sciences of action' (Weber 1978: 4).

In course of time, as I entered deeper into the problems of agrarian classes and the backward castes, I found it difficult to turn my back on matters of policy. And, of course, there was the example of Max Weber who was associated with both the Verein für Sozialpolitik (Association for Social Policy) and the Evangelische-Soziale Kongress (Evangelical-Social Congress). It was the same Weber who had insisted that sociology was an 'empirical' and not a 'dogmatic' science.

These considerations have led me to make the distinction between policy analysis and policy prescription. It is an important distinction, although no honest sociologist will say that the distinction is easy to maintain consistently in practice. Here I ought to say that the scope of sociological enquiry extends far beyond matters of policy. Some institutions operate without being affected directly or substantially by policy interventions whereas others are palpably affected by them. The latter has been the case with the universities in the last 50 to 60 years throughout the world, and particularly in India. No one who studies the university in India today can ignore the changes taking place in it, or the fact that many of them arise directly from policies adopted by the authorities responsible for its maintenance and care.

To the extent that policies palpably affect the operation and transformation of institutions, they are legitimate subjects of sociological enquiry. Social policy, like any other form of social action, has unintended consequences, and an important part of sociological analysis is to identify and reveal the disjunction between the intentions that create an act and its consequences. But what the sociologist does best is to reveal the disjunction *after* the act has been completed. Can he employ the tools of his craft and his professional acumen to *anticipate* the disjunctions that are likely to take place? In other words, how far can he anticipate the consequences of a particular act and foretell that the intention behind it is likely to be defeated? It is here that value judgements and judgements of reality become entangled with each other, and personal preferences displace scholarly judgement.

I have not been much involved personally with the making of academic policy except, briefly, as the chairman of the Indian Council of Social Science Research and, even more briefly, as a member of the National Knowledge Commission. Those experiences made me appreciate the need for informed policy in the pursuit of science and scholarship and, at the same time, confirmed my scepticism about the outcome of such policies in our present social and political circumstances. While scholars and scientists never tire of stressing the value of autonomy, they are careless about anticipating the consequences of policies of the kind that repeatedly, not to say inevitably, undermine that autonomy. In their dealings with the powers, they are generally eager to please, and lull their critical abilities with the thought that nothing in institutional life can be guaranteed to fail—or to succeed.

I have learnt much about the relationship between the intellectuals and the powers, and the threats confronting the institutions of science and scholarship from my association with Edward Shils who wrote extensively on these subjects (Shils 1972, 1997). I made his acquaintance fairly early in my academic career when he was associated with the work of the Education Commission of India (Shils 2006: 103–4). Sometime in 1979, he gave me his Jefferson Lectures on the relations between universities, government, and society, and I was much impressed by what I read. He also encouraged me to publish in *Minerva* which, in his own words, he edited 'with great severity'. He had an overbearing manner and a sharp tongue, and I had been warned against his domineering ways by colleagues at both Cambridge and Chicago, but I found him remarkably forbearing in his dealings with me.

I believe that no sociologist since Max Weber has written with as much insight and passion about universities as Shils, and he wrote much more extensively on the subject than Weber. My last meeting with him was on the occasion of the roundtable on universities of the twenty-first century, whose proceedings were published in *Minerva*, vol. XXX, no. 2, Summer 1992. He spoke on 'The Service of Society and the Advancement of Learning in the Twenty-First Century', and in his speech castigated the authorities of the universities for the many compromises they had made. He said, 'I do not foresee the emergence of a generation of courageous and intelligent university presidents, provosts and deans who can render discriminating judgements when they have to approve or disapprove of appointments proposed by departments' (Shils 1992: 267).

When I went to see him in his apartment after the event, he appeared tired and a little dejected. Perhaps he felt that the barbarians were close to the gate and that they could not be held back for very long. The work of Edward Shils has much to say to those who wish to learn about universities in the contemporary world, whether in the United States or in India, and I have come to regard him as a mentor. I dedicate this book to his memory as a small token of my admiration for the courage with which he spoke his mind on difficult and controversial subjects.

References

Béteille, André. 1965. *Caste, Class and Power.* Berkeley: University of California Press.

———. 1981. 'The Indian University: Academic Standards and the Pursuit of Equality', *Minerva*, vol. xxx, no. 2, pp. 282–310.

———. 2000a. *Antinomies of Society.* New Delhi: Oxford University Press.

———. 2000b. *Chronicles of Our Time.* New Delhi: Penguin Books.

———. 2005. *Ideology and Social Science.* New Delhi: Penguin Books.

Shils, Edward. 1972. *The Intellectuals and the Powers.* Chicago: University of Chicago Press.

———. 1992. 'The Service of Society and the Advancement of Learning in the Twenty-First Century'. *Minerva*, vol. XXX, no. 2, pp. 242–68.

———. 1997. *The Calling of Education.* Chicago: University of Chicago Press.

———. 2006. *A Fragment of a Sociological Autobiography.* New Brunswick: Transaction Publishers.

Srinivas, M.N. 1952. *Religion and Society among the Coorgs.* Oxford: Clarendon Press.

Weber, Max. 1978. *Economy and Society.* Berkeley: University of California Press.

Chapter 1

Universities and Society*

The annual convocation is a very special event in the life of a university. It provides an occasion for the symbolic expression of the university as a community. This year's sesquicentennial convocation is of more than ordinary significance, for with it the university enters the hundred and fiftieth year of its existence. I am deeply touched that you have asked me to be with you today and to deliver the convocation address. It seems only the other day when I entered the university as a student. I could scarcely imagine then that I would be asked to address a gathering of this nature.

The University of Calcutta was established at a time of transition not only in the development of knowledge but also in the growth of institutions. New branches of learning were coming into being and new centres for their cultivation being established. In the past, there were only a few universities, and they were small and socially exclusive. The whole of England had only two universities until the beginning of the nineteenth century, and they were not open to women or to those who were outside the established church. By contrast, the University of Calcutta is a modern university in the sense that it is an open and secular institution.

*This is the text of the convocation address delivered at the University of Calcutta in 2006.

The idea of a university as an open and secular institution would have appeared strange at the beginning or even in the middle of the nineteenth century in most parts of the world, including Europe and America. We have come a long way to be able to take for granted that a university should not be regulated by religious rules or religious authority, and that it should be open to all classes and communities, and to women as well as men. The creation of a new type of institution is as significant a departure in the life of society as the creation of any new branch of learning, whether in the sciences or the humanities.

Perhaps I can explain what I mean by going back to a convocation address given at this university in 1866 by Sir Henry Maine who was one of its early vice-chancellors. Maine had said, 'The fact is that the founders of the University of Calcutta thought to create an *aristocratic* institution; and in spite of themselves, they created a *popular* institution' (Banerjee et al. 1957: 127 [emphasis in original]). In the 1850s, it would be natural for those who wished to set up a new university, whether in India or in England, to plan for a small and exclusive institution. The universities of the past were designed for the select few, not the general populace. This is no longer the case. I am not sure how well Maine read the signs of the future, for they were not very clear at that time.

Maine himself was a distinguished academic who had served as a professor at both Oxford and Cambridge, two of the oldest universities in the world. He, therefore, knew at first hand what the universities were like in the middle of the nineteenth century. They were on the whole conservative places, both academically and socially, and were only gradually breaking out of the hierarchical mould in which they had been set for centuries. Today they are modern universities, but what I would like to stress is that they did not become open and secular institutions in a year or a decade.

As a sociologist and social anthropologist, I have been struck by the fact that Sir Herbert Spencer and Sir E.B. Tylor, two of the founding fathers of these related disciplines, failed to secure a university education because they were both religious dissenters. In their time, both Oxford and Cambridge restricted admission even within the Christian faith to only those who subscribed to the Thirty-nine Articles of the Church of England, that is, the established church. These restrictions remained in place until well into the second half of the nineteenth century.

The admission of women into the universities was a slow, halting, and uneven process. Until the end of the nineteenth century, the universities were male preserves, in practice in most places and in principle in many. Oxford and Cambridge have colleges that go back to the thirteenth and the fourteenth centuries, but the first women's colleges were established there only in the second half of the nineteenth century. Even after women students were enrolled in them, they were not at first permitted to take the examinations of the university; and when they were later permitted to do that, they were still made to wait before they could be admitted to the degrees of the university. Today, of course, the presence of women, as both students and teachers, is taken for granted in most universities in the world.

* * *

Our universities at Calcutta, Bombay, and Madras did not carry from the medieval past the heavy baggage of hierarchical customs, practices, and traditions. They were open and secular institutions from almost the start, at least in orientation, if not in every particular practice. It took Oxford and Cambridge several centuries to admit women to their degrees; at Calcutta it took hardly a couple of decades.

If we look back at the third quarter of the nineteenth century, we will be struck by the contrast between the older universities in England and the new ones that were emerging in the Presidency capitals in India. In England, France, and Germany, changes in social outlook and orientation began largely outside the universities which responded to those changes slowly and often reluctantly. In India, it was the other way around. The wider society remained set in the hierarchical mould of kinship, caste, and religion while the universities, as open and secular institutions, were in the forefront in creating a new social outlook and orientation.

I am well aware that the first three universities in India were set up under colonial rule, and those responsible for setting them up had their own plans and their own intentions. But as a sociologist, I am less interested in the intentions of those who set up the universities than in the consequences of their actions; for it is a truism in sociology that the consequences of human action are often different, and sometimes very different, from the intentions of the actors. If we believe that open and secular institutions are essential for the health and well-being of civil society, we must acknowledge that the long-term consequences of setting up new universities and new medical and law colleges, under no matter what auspices, have been momentous.

Throughout the nineteenth century and well into the twentieth, the universities in India were few and far between, and they were generally very small in size. They were islands in a country the vast majority of whose population went without the benefit of elementary education and even literacy. Those who were responsible for the care of the universities did not in that age think that university education was for the masses. University education became socially significant not because it reached into every corner of the country but because, as open and secular institutions, the universities served as exemplars and models of a new kind of social existence.

Those who came to the universities and their colleges in the nineteenth and early decades of the twentieth centuries were predominantly from the upper castes and they were predominantly men. This was not because the universities excluded women or members of the lower castes, but because the society from which they drew their students and teachers was hierarchical and patriarchal. University education did not change society directly or all at once, but it planted the seeds of change in it. The universities provided fertile breeding grounds for a new ideal of social life and produced the men and women who would later carry that ideal forward.

Although the universities were places of equal opportunity in a sense, the opportunities actually available within them were very few in comparison to the scale and diversity of society as a whole. Further, the few opportunities they did provide were generally seized by those who were already advantaged. In a society in which life chances are very unevenly distributed, equality of opportunity depends not simply on the removal of disabilities but also on the creation of abilities (Tawney 1964: 103–4). The promotion of equality as an active social policy was not a basic objective of the nineteenth century university in India or anywhere. In his Jefferson Lectures, Edward Shils (1979: 134) had pointed out that the idea that 'universities could create social equality' was a very new one. The colonial government succeeded in introducing some institutional innovation, but a radical transformation of the hierarchical order of Indian society was outside its purview.

Things changed when India became independent in 1947. The first prime minister of India, Jawaharlal Nehru (1981: 521), pointed to the contradiction between the ideal of equality and the pervasive practice of inequality, and said, 'In India, at any rate, we must aim at equality.' The new constitution, adopted in 1950, gave the government a different mandate from what any colonial government enjoyed. Strong provisions for equality were written into the part on Fundamental Rights as well as the one on Directive Principles of State Policy. There were tensions between the different equality provisions which came to light in course of time, but the constitutional mandate was clearly for 'equality of status and of opportunity'.

The leaders of independent India wanted a more active role for the universities in the transformation of Indian society. The Education Commission set up under Dr D.S. Kothari observed, 'If this "change on a grand scale" is to be achieved without violent revolution (and even for that it would be necessary) there is one instrument, and one instrument only, that can be used: EDUCATION' (Government of India 1971: 8). An earlier Commission, set up under Dr S. Radhakrishnan in 1948, also sought a more active role for the universities in the transformation of society. It said, 'Education is a universal right, not a class privilege' (Government of India 1950: 50). This is a far more ambitious objective than the one with which the first universities were set up 150 years ago.

An all-round expansion of higher education began almost immediately after independence. Existing universities and colleges increased the enrolment of students and the appointment of teachers, and new ones were established in the different parts of the country. An important consideration in the expansion of higher education after independence was the need to ensure that no part of the country remained without its own universities and colleges. Women in particular have benefited from this since travelling long distances was and still remains a deterrent against their entry into colleges and universities.

The preponderance of some sections of society over others in the social composition of the university appeared increasingly worrisome to planners and policymakers under the new dispensation. But, as one would expect in a country with the size and diversity of India, the pattern of development was not the same everywhere. In some regions, social and political movements had led to the creation of institutions to meet the needs of religious minorities and socially and educationally backward communities even before independence.

The incorporation of women into the social life of the university was slow and it followed an uneven course. As I have noted, the idea that women should be admitted into the institutions of higher learning was a new one even in the industrially advanced countries just a hundred years ago. In a markedly patriarchal society such as ours, it was likely to encounter strong resistance from the family and the community even when the state was sympathetic to it. It was considered natural to have separate undergraduate colleges for men and women, and until quite recent times postgraduate departments had few women students and even fewer women teachers. And the women who entered the universities came mainly from the middle and the upper-middle classes and from families which had already had some exposure to higher education.

There are now many more mixed colleges and many more women in postgraduate departments than at the time of independence. The university has been a pioneer in the creation of a new basis for the relationship between men and women in India. Young men and women unrelated by ties of kinship and community have been able to interact more freely there than perhaps in any other domain of society. In the past, in all social classes, a woman was already burdened by the cares of domestic life by the time she was 17 or 18; today, if she has the luck to enter a college or a university, a new life might open up for her at that age.

Success in academic competition creates a new sense of confidence in women, although we must not exaggerate the extent of change that this brings about in the actual relations between men and women. Ours is still a deeply conservative society and conservatism takes its most obdurate form in the attitudes of men towards women. Academic and other achievements do not automatically bring about equality in social relations, and women are reminded at every turn of their subordinate position in the family and the community. Yet it is true that the best women undergraduates generally prefer mixed colleges for their study to colleges only for women. This is a far cry from where things stood only a hundred years ago.

Today the universities and colleges are also much more mixed in their caste composition. Students and teachers no longer come to them from only a handful of privileged castes and communities. The processes through which this kind of diversity has come about are somewhat different from those by which larger numbers of women have been incorporated into the university system. Here government and politics have played a more direct part in making the system socially more inclusive.

* * *

The tendency for public institutions to become socially inclusive emerged in the nineteenth century and gathered momentum during that century. In some countries, the tendency first appeared outside the universities which lagged behind for some time; in others, the universities were in the forefront while other parts of society remained apathetic and resistant. Perhaps it was a fortunate accident that the first universities were established in India at an important turning point in institutional life. The tendency towards the development of open and secular institutions appears in retrospect as a secular one and it is perhaps irreversible. But it started later in some countries than in others, and the social environment in which it operates is not equally favourable everywhere.

While a modern university must aim at being inclusive, the degree of its inclusiveness cannot be the only measure of its success. As a public institution in a democratic society, it must be socially inclusive; but as a centre of teaching and research, it must be academically discriminating. A university or college that is indifferent to the quality of its teachers or the performance of its students fails to meet its obligations to society. In a university, the objective of social inclusiveness cannot be promoted without consideration of success or failure in the pursuit of science and scholarship.

The first University Education Commission in independent India had observed, 'Intellectual work is not for all, it is only for the intellectually competent' (Government of India 1950: 98). Its chairman was Dr S. Radhakrishnan who had been a professor at the University of Calcutta. We must ask ourselves if the universities today are able to maintain levels of competence, not to mention standards of excellence, that would pass muster with the professors of his generation. The material resources available to them were slender even in comparison with our material resources today. They made up for this lack by their commitment to the rigorous demands of science and scholarship. We can hardly discuss in a serious way the responsibilities of the university as a public institution if we fail to distinguish between unwarranted exclusion on social grounds and justifiable discrimination on academic ones.

A policy to make the universities fully inclusive socially may not lead to an immediate and significant change in their social composition, particularly in a society with many classes and communities whose individual members are very unequally endowed with social, cultural, and intellectual capital. India at the time of independence provides a clear example of this. Dalits, Muslims, and women were not debarred from entering the universities as their counterparts would have been till the middle of the nineteenth century in Oxford and Cambridge, but they did not in fact enter them in sufficient numbers. This happened either because they lacked the preliminary educational qualifications for entry or because they stayed away due to social pressures from the family and the community. After independence the government began to play a more active part in opening up the universities to all sections of society, and pressures from below began to make themselves felt towards the same end. This came to be viewed in a broad sense as the democratization of the universities.

The democratization of the Indian university has not always been a smooth and orderly process, and it has had unanticipated consequences, not all of them conducive to the pursuit of study and research. Pressures to accommodate new classes and communities have led to rapid and sometimes reckless expansion of the institutions of learning. New undergraduate colleges, new postgraduate departments, and new universities have been opened without due consideration of the resources available for their proper functioning. Academic standards have been relaxed, sometimes abruptly and even arbitrarily, in the name of equality and justice through decisions taken outside the universities by persons with little experience or knowledge of science and scholarship.

It is true that when universities become socially more inclusive, in the long run they also gain academically. This is what happened in the European universities between the middle of the nineteenth century and the middle of the twentieth. As new classes and communities are accommodated in the universities, they bring in fresh talent and fresh experience. But this happy outcome depends to a large extent on the process through which they become socially inclusive and the forces by which that process is driven. When the drive to become socially inclusive leads to a sudden and dramatic increase in numbers without any corresponding growth in material and intellectual resources, academic standards are bound to become unsettled and be placed in jeopardy. It will be difficult to deny that this is what happened in one Indian university after another in the 1960s, 1970s, and 1980s.

Universities cannot become socially more inclusive and at the same time maintain and enhance their academic standards unless the supply of the talent on which they depend is continuously augmented. They can either wait for a gradual but assured improvement in elementary and secondary education or take the short cut of raising admissions and appointments by relaxing their academic standards. In Europe and America, the universities became socially more inclusive and simultaneously raised their standards because attention was paid all the time to a steady expansion and improvement of elementary and secondary education. In India this was not done in the early decades of independence, and the colleges and universities are now paying the price for the neglect of school education.

The ideal of the university as an ivory tower is no longer viable in the modern world. No university in a democratic country can insulate itself fully from the social and political currents that swirl around it. The process of rigorous academic selection affects members of some sections of society more adversely than those of others. Those who are adversely affected find it natural to believe that they are victims not of academic but of social discrimination. The political articulation of that belief persistently and aggressively can undermine the university's confidence in its own moral integrity. It will be idle to maintain that in this atmosphere, the authorities of the university can exercise their academic judgement calmly, and without fear or favour.

The building of open and secular institutions that are socially inclusive and yet do not lose sight of their fundamental aims and objectives is not an easy undertaking. In the case of universities, the undertaking cannot be pursued successfully if we wish out of existence the deep and pervasive tensions between the demands of social inclusion and those of academic discrimination. Making the universities socially inclusive is of the utmost importance. But there are no short cuts to it. If we attempt too many short cuts, we may subvert the very purpose for which universities exist, which is the pursuit of science and scholarship through disciplined teaching and research.

References

Banerjee, Pramathanath et al. 1957. *Hundred Years of the University of Calcutta*. Calcutta: University of Calcutta Press.

Government of India. 1950. *The Report of the University Education Commission, 1948–49*. New Delhi: Ministry of Education.

———. 1971. *Education and National Development: Report of the Education Commission, 1964–66*. New Delhi: NCERT.

Nehru, Jawaharlal. 1981. *The Discovery of India*. New Delhi: Jawaharlal Nehru Memorial Fund.

Shils, Edward. 1979. 'Government and Universities in the United States', *Minerva*, vol. XVII, no. 1, pp. 129–71.

Tawney, R.H. 1964. *Equality*. London: Unwin Books.

Chapter 2

Universities as Public Institutions*

It is natural for someone who has spent the better part of his life in a university to speak well of the universities, at least in public. But there was a time in India when others too spoke well of them. Pre-eminent among them was India's first prime minister, Jawaharlal Nehru. In a convocation address delivered at Allahabad University just after independence, he dwelt upon the role of knowledge in human advancement and pointed to the things for which a modern university stands. He added, 'If the universities discharge their duty adequately, then it is well with the nation and the people' (Nehru 1958: 333).

Nobody can maintain that our universities have met all the expectations placed on them at the time of independence. They have grown enormously in the years since independence, and their growth has been disorderly and often in response to pressures that are far removed from the ideals of scholarship, humanism, and civility for which Nehru believed the universities ought to stand. It has become a matter of routine to speak of crises on the campus. Nothing will be gained by seeking to minimize the disorder that characterizes our universities today, or by saying that such disorder has been a common feature of universities all over the world in the second half of the twentieth century.

*This is the text of the G. Ram Reddy Memorial Lecture delivered at Hyderabad in 2005. It was subsequently published in *Economic and Political Weekly*, vol. XL, no. 31, 30 July 2005, pp. 3377–81.

However, if we are to understand the place of the university in society, we have to take a broader view of both university and society and see their relationship over a longer span of time. Universities are not only centres of learning, however badly or well they play their part in the transmission and creation of knowledge, they are also social institutions that provide the setting for a very distinctive kind of interaction among young men and women, and between the generations (see Chapter 1). Here we will try to examine the social significance of the university as well as its contribution to the advancement of learning.

The universities may act as bastions of traditional and conservative values, as they did in Europe for much of their existence during the Middle Ages and even later; or, they may provide the setting for a new kind of social imagination and experience, as they did when they were first established in India in the second half of the nineteenth century. I will argue that the Indian university has played a significant part in the education for democratic citizenship, although this education, which began more than 150 years ago, has not by any means been completed.

* * *

The nineteenth century witnessed great change and innovation in the institutional foundations of higher learning in different parts of the world. The changes were all associated, in one way or another, directly or indirectly, with the displacement of a hierarchical by a democratic legal, political, and social order. They took place in many different countries but not all at once or in the same way everywhere. In some countries, notably France, and to some extent also Germany, the changes were rapid and dramatic, whereas in others, such as England, they were slow and gradual. Where universities had existed before, they were often overhauled; where they had not existed before, new ones were brought into being.

The reconstitution of the institutions of higher learning began in Europe at the turn of the eighteenth century. The reforms took somewhat different forms in France and Germany. The changes in France were more radical. Although they had their beginnings before the Revolution, the real architect of the new system was Napoleon. What he sought to do was not so much to reform the universities, which in France were then in a moribund state, as to create institutional alternatives to them. These institutional alternatives were the *grandes écoles* or 'great schools' of which, historically, the two most important were the *École Polytechnique* set up in 1794 to train engineers for the civil and military services and the *École Normale Superieure* set up in 1795 to train teachers for state secondary schools.

In Germany, reconstitution was less dramatic. It began with the establishment under Wilhelm von Humboldt of a new type of university in Berlin in 1810 based on the principle of Einheit der Lehre und Forschung or the unity of teaching and research. Humboldt wanted the universities to be engaged not only in the assimilation, criticism, and transmission of existing knowledge but also to become centres for the creation of new knowledge. Under his inspiration, the German universities became the most advanced universities in the world. In course of time the German model extended its influence to the United States where the first 'research university', Johns Hopkins, was established in 1876.

Although they were not universities in the true sense of the term, the *grandes écoles* introduced principles of institutional organization that were radically new in their time, but have now come to be accepted widely if not universally. They were open and secular institutions and in that sense different from the universities of the past and in advance of the universities of their time, including the German ones.

The *grandes écoles* were designed to give effect to Napoleon's ideal of 'careers open to talent'. It cannot be too strongly emphasized that the idea of careers open to talent, whether in education or in employment, was a radically new one even in Europe 200 years ago. It permeated all kinds of institutions in the course of the nineteenth and the twentieth centuries and gradually became commonplace in one country after another. In the past, recruitment in both education and employment was governed to a far greater extent by birth and patronage than by merit or ability. Napoleon set out to change all this, and achieved success, though only in the long run.

In earlier times, the universities such as those at Paris, Oxford, and Cambridge, were regulated largely by religious rules and religious authority. The dissociation of the European universities from the church was a slow and long-drawn process. The *grandes écoles* were pioneers in being largely secular in their orientation and organization. The universities in Europe and elsewhere gradually began to follow the course charted out by them. Today, if we take it for granted that the modern university should be a secular institution, we must not forget that the idea was a new one even in the nineteenth century.

Education and employment came to be linked together through the idea of the career. Napoleon set a very high value on education and training in the formation of public servants. Along with the great schools there grew the 'great services' or the *grands corps*, recruitment to both of which came to be based on open, national competition. All of this was begun at a time when the universities of Oxford and Cambridge were still closely tied to the hierarchies of the church, and recruitment to the civil and military services in England was still largely through patronage. This was to change in the 1850s with the Trevelyan–Northcote reforms, which created a new type of civil servant known in the Indian Civil Service as the 'competition wallah' (Trevelyan 1964). The universities too began to change in England at about the same time.

* * *

Even though there is a long tradition in India of the cultivation and transmission of specialized and systematic knowledge, what we know as the universities today had their beginnings only in the middle of the nineteenth century. It was pointed out by the Education Commission of 1964–6 that the universities with which it was concerned had very little genealogical or historical connection with India's 'ancient and medieval centres of learning' (Education Commission 1971: 8). The first modern universities that were established in Calcutta, Bombay, and Madras in 1857 did not carry with them the hierarchical baggage of medieval institutions. As we have seen, this was a time of major reconstitution in the institutions of learning in the West. The Indian universities were almost from the beginning open and secular institutions. They were among the first such institutions in the country, and as such have had a social and not just an intellectual significance far in excess of their size and material resources.

Indians who entered the colleges and universities in the nineteenth century encountered a whole new world of ideas to which access was mainly through a new language. Educated Indians had been used to operating through more than one language. If they were upper-caste Hindus, it would not be unusual for them to know some Sanskrit and a little Persian in addition to the language of the home. But exploring the world through the English language was a new kind of experience. The Indian intellectual tradition, which had once been active and vibrant, had become stagnant and moribund by the end of the eighteenth century. The encounter with Western ideas in the new centres of learning released a flood of dormant intellectual energy.

A whole array of new subjects and new approaches to them came into view. It is a characteristic of modern universities, in contrast to traditional centres of learning, that new branches of knowledge are continuously added and explored in them. It has sometimes been said that the fascination with Western learning led to the neglect and even the denigration of traditional forms of knowledge, including much that was of value in it. While this may be to some extent true, no deliberate attempt was generally made to abolish the study of classical languages, classical philosophy, or ancient and medieval history in the new centres of learning.

The Brahminical tradition of learning was not only narrowly focused intellectually, it was also socially very exclusive. Women and members of the lower castes had little or no access to it. The new centres of learning—the colleges and the universities—opened up new fields of knowledge, and also opened their doors to excluded sections of society.

Family background had an acknowledged place in the classification of students in Oxford, and the following categories were officially used: *baronis filius* (sons of noblemen), *equitis filius* (sons of knights), *armigeri filius* (sons of esquires), *generosi filius* (sons of gentlemen), *plebei filius* (sons of commoners), and *clerici filius* (sons of clergymen). In keeping with traditional distinctions of status, sons of bishops were listed with sons of noblemen, not of clergymen. Those of inferior social status paid smaller fees, but those of superior status were entitled to take the first degree after nine instead of twelve terms of residence. It is noteworthy that these categories were used until as late as 1891 when the Registrar of Oxford began to record the father's occupation instead of his status. In Cambridge, the privilege whereby sons of noblemen were excused from taking examinations (the *jus natalium*) was abolished only in 1884 (Rashdall 1936: 470).

The marks of invidious social (as opposed to academic) distinction were visible also in the internal structure of the college. There were the distinctions, first, between master, fellows, and students. 'Students' themselves were of various categories. The core consisted of the 'scholars' who, like the fellows, were supported by the foundation: the college provided them with education as well as bed and board.

But there were others who had to pay for what the college gave them. These included 'pensioners' who were ordinary fee-paying students in residence, and 'fellow commoners' who paid extra and had the privilege of dining with the fellows. At the bottom were the 'sizars' who, in Cambridge, were granted the benefits of college life, including college education, in return for menial services rendered to the more privileged members of the college (Stone 1974, vol. 1: chapters I and III).

The hierarchical structures of universities such as Cambridge, Oxford, and Paris reflected the values of the medieval societies in which they had originated and grown. From the end of the eighteenth century onwards, those societies began to change in the direction of greater equality. What I wish to emphasize here is that in England, France, and Germany, the universities responded to changes in attitudes and values that first began elsewhere in the wider society. In India it was the opposite. The wider society began to respond, slowly and not always effectively, to changes that were initiated in the colleges, universities, and a small number of other modern institutions. In other words, in India the universities were in advance of society whereas in the West they had fallen behind.

In contrast to the universities of the past, which were socially exclusive, the modern university is socially inclusive. The Indian university admits students and appoints teachers generally without consideration of race, caste, creed, or gender. This is by and large true today of most modern universities. The emergence of modern institutions has been a slow and in many places a painful process. But they constitute the core of civil society and are essential for the creation and sustenance of universal citizenship, on the one hand, and the constitutional state, on the other.

In the past, universities restricted admission on grounds of religion. This was natural in a world where the institutions of learning were regulated by religious rules and religious authority. Until the second half of the nineteenth century, Oxford and Cambridge required students as well as teachers to subscribe to the 39 Articles of the Church of England. It is well known that both Herbert Spencer, the most famous British sociologist of the nineteenth century and E.B. Tylor, widely regarded as the father of British anthropology, went without a university education as they were religious dissenters.

The most striking change in the social composition and character of the universities came when they opened their doors to women. Until well into the nineteenth century, universities and other institutions of higher learning were male preserves. As far as such institutions went, women were largely invisible, except occasionally as servants. Even the *grandes écoles* in France, which were undoubtedly ahead of their time, remained male preserves throughout the nineteenth century: careers open to talent meant careers open to male talent only.

Resistance to the entry of women took much time and effort to wear down in the older European universities. Cambridge provides a good example. Permission was granted for the opening of two colleges for women, Girton and Newnham, only in the second half of the nineteenth century. But, although women were allowed to study in these colleges, they were not allowed to take examinations of the University of Cambridge. Then they were allowed to take the examinations but not admitted to the degrees of the university. It was only in the twentieth century that women were enabled to acquire full membership of the university as both students and teachers.

In the late nineteenth and early twentieth centuries, women came to the universities in very small numbers and mainly from well-to-do upper-caste families. Now they come in larger numbers and from a variety of castes and communities, although they are still outnumbered by men, and all castes and communities are not equally represented among them. If any thing, there is a larger upper-caste bias among women than men, and this is true for students as well as teachers.

In India, the university and the college have played a more significant part in the social emancipation of women than any other public institution. Women have by now competed successfully for the best prizes in university examinations and the highest positions in faculty appointments, not in every university or in every faculty perhaps, but in a sufficient number of places for them to be able to feel secure about their academic achievements within the university. The success of women is particularly visible in the better metropolitan universities, whether we take the universities of Calcutta and Bombay among the older ones or Delhi University and Jawaharlal Nehru University among the newer. All of this has been accompanied by a marked change in the social participation of women in the universities whether as students or as teachers. For women, even more than for men, the university is not only a place of work; it is also a place of recreation, and, for some women, perhaps the only place of recreation. There is more equality between men and women in both performance and participation in the university than anywhere outside. But we must see this transformation for what it is: it is largely a middle-class phenomenon although the middle class has been expanding steadily and continuously in recent decades.

The very idea of the career woman would be impossible without the college or the university. To be sure, women worked in the household and on the farm in the past. But household work was confining and women's work on the farm was generally both onerous and degrading. It is in the modern office, more than anywhere else, that college- or university-educated women are able to work with men as their equals and sometimes as their superiors.

Young men and women unrelated by ties of kinship and community can interact more freely in the university than perhaps in any other domain in society. If this has done nothing else, it has at the very least created a new basis for the relationship between men and women in contemporary India. In the past, whether among Hindus or Muslims, the life led by women was either hard or confined, or both, and that is probably true for most women even today. It is mainly in the college and the university that, as a young adult, a woman can enjoy a little freedom to explore new social relations and to construct a new social identity. In the past, in all social classes a woman was already burdened by the cares of domestic life by the time she was 16 or 17; today, if she has the luck to enter a university, a new life might open up for her at that age. The university has provided a new ideal of womanhood even if only a handful of women are able to give shape and substance to that ideal.

The modern university provides a setting for a new kind of interchange not only between men and women but also among persons belonging to different castes and communities. The barriers of language, religion, and caste can be overcome relatively easily in such a setting, although here identity politics can also reinforce the boundaries between communities instead of softening them. It is far from my intention to suggest that because modern institutions provide opportunities for individuals to interact on a new basis, those institutions can be guaranteed to operate without friction. No large and complex society can reconstitute itself without experiencing conflict and disorder, and if the universities appear embattled, it is partly because they are in the forefront of this reconstitution.

* * *

While a modern university must strive actively and continuously to be socially inclusive, it must be academically discriminating in the treatment of its members. A university or college which is indifferent to the quality of its teachers and the performance of its students cannot be said to fulfil its obligations as a centre of learning. In a university the objective of social inclusiveness cannot be promoted without consideration of success or failure in academic performance. In looking at our universities today, we cannot wish out of existence the real and pervasive tensions between the demands of social inclusiveness and those of academic excellence.

The University Education Commission under Dr S. Radhakrishnan observed: 'Intellectual work is not for all, it is only for the intellectually competent' (Government of India 1950: 98). Today, on an occasion like this, it is important to remember not only Mr Nehru but also Dr Radhakrishnan, for those who are responsible for the governance of universities are often willing to compromise academic standards for fear of being denounced as elitists. We can hardly discuss the responsibilities of universities as public institutions in a serious way if we fail to distinguish between unwarranted exclusion on social grounds and justifiable discrimination on academic grounds.

Napoleon's ideal of 'careers open to talent' was frankly meritocratic in its orientation and he would not fight shy of creating an elite, provided it was an elite based on merit and not birth. Many changes in outlook and orientation have taken place in the 200 years since Napoleon's time. Social scientists (Arrow et al. 2001) and philosophers (Rawls 1973) have raised serious questions about the costs as well as the benefits of meritocracy. Rawls has associated the principles of careers open to talent with what he has called a 'callous meritocratic society'. In this view, the single-minded pursuit of merit at the expense of all other values is detrimental to the health and well-being of society.

It has been pointed out by more than one author that the concept of 'merit' is ambiguous and difficult to define. A meritocracy may be viewed as a system which carries the meritarian principle to its extreme limit by excluding all other social principles such as amity, compassion, moderation, and tolerance. But one does not need to be an advocate of meritocracy in order to appreciate and support the principle of selection by merit rather than some inherited attribute. It is true that there is no agreed definition of merit and that it means different things to different persons; but that hardly settles the issue. Most things that are of value are difficult to define, but that does not mean that we cannot take them into account in the operation of institutions. Critics of the meritarian principle often say that what should count in the distribution of benefits and burdens is not merit but need (Sen 1973). Need should indeed be a consideration of first importance; but then it is no more easy to define need than it is to define merit, for different people have different conceptions not only of merit but also of need.

One does not require a general, formal, and abstract definition of merit in order to grade MA examination papers in history or to select lecturers in physics or economics without fear or favour and in accordance with academic criteria agreed upon in advance. If merit is given short shrift in such cases, as it often is in India, it is not always in order to meet some higher social objective but for the pettiest and the most mundane of reasons. A public institution, whether it is a university, a hospital, or a bank, has specific functions to perform and appointments to such institutions cannot be made without consideration of ability and performance in the discharge of particular responsibilities. It is in this context that discrimination has to be applied in admissions and appointments in a university, no matter how socially inclusive it may aim to be.

A university cannot discharge its responsibilities to society unless it remains vigilant in maintaining and improving its academic standards, although these need not be the same everywhere. Universities differ enormously in their material as well as human resources. Such disparities exist not only between different countries but also between different universities in the same country. It would be foolish to expect a small university in a remote part of India to have the same material and intellectual capital as a wealthy private university, such as Harvard or Stanford, in a rich country. But again, if there are no resources or if the resources are manifestly inadequate, it may be imprudent to start a university simply because there is a 'social' need for it, and hope that it will somehow run itself.

Every university need not be assessed by the same standards of academic excellence. Indeed, it is of the essence of a university as an autonomous institution that it should, within a broad understanding of what universities should do, set its own academic standards. To apply the same standards mechanically in every case, without consideration of the disparities in resources between institutions would hardly be reasonable. A university should be free to set its own academic standards after due consideration of the resources available to it; but having set those standards, it cannot suffer them to be treated with indifference or neglect in evaluating the performance of its students and teachers.

Given the variations and changes in the resources with which they have to work, universities cannot adopt a rigid and inflexible attitude to academic standards, whether in teaching or in research. Even the balance between teaching and research need not be the same in every university. The manner in which teaching is conducted will depend on the ratio of students to teachers in the college or university concerned, and the scale on which research is undertaken will depend on the funds at its disposal for research. There is nothing wrong if a university with limited resources decides to devote more of those resources to teaching than to research, provided it is recognized that teaching itself suffers in the long run if research is completely neglected.

Flexibility in the determination by a university of its own academic standards should not lead to laxity in the application of the standards it has adopted for itself. A university with limited resources which adopts modest academic standards to which it adheres scrupulously is to be much preferred to one which has larger resources and adopts elevated standards which its members persistently disregard with impunity.

Thus, academic standards are neither invariant nor unalterable. They change with changes in the volume and diversity of knowledge and also with changes in the size and composition of the institutions of learning. In the last 200 years, universities have grown in number and size and have become increasingly diverse in their social composition.

As I have already indicated, the tendency for universities to become socially more and more inclusive is a secular one, and it is probably also irreversible. The tendency began to manifest itself about 200 years ago, although in most countries it began to gather momentum less than a hundred years ago. Where it started late, it was often driven by political pressure and by state policy.

Maine did no more than to speak of the university as a popular institution. After independence, government and politics began to take a hand in making them actually so, but they did not always pay heed to the academic costs that this imposed on the universities.

References

Arrow, K., S. Bowles, and S. Durlauf (eds). 2001. *Meritocracy and Economic Inequality*. New Delhi: Oxford University Press.

Education Commission. 1971. *Education and National Development*, vol. 1. New Delhi: NCERT.

Government of India. 1950. *The Report of the University Education Commission, 1948–49*, vol. 1. New Delhi: Ministry of Education.

Nehru, Jawaharlal. 1958. *Speeches, 1946–49*, vol. 1. New Delhi: Government of India.

Rashdall, Hastings. 1936. *The Universities of Europe in the Middle Ages*, vol 1. London: Oxford University Press.

Rawls, John. 1973. *A Theory of Justice*. London: Oxford University Press.

Sen, Amartya. 1973. *On Economic Inequality*. Oxford: Basil Blackwell.

Stone, Lawrence (ed.). 1974. *The University in Society*, 2 vols. Princeton: Princeton University Press.

Trevelyan, G.O. 1964. *The Competition Wallah*. London: Macmillan.

Chapter 3

The Expansion of Universities*

The universities in India have grown continuously in number and size during the last hundred years. The growth was slow at first but it acquired momentum with the passage of time. There were very few universities to begin with and they were small and exclusive. They were islands for the pursuit of advanced study in a country of very large size, the vast majority of whose population were unschooled or even unlettered. The colonial government, at whose initiative the first universities were set up, did not aim at using them to bring about a social revolution in the country. Yet, its decision to set them up had unintended and unforeseen consequences of some significance.

The advent of independence led to a spurt in the growth of colleges and universities throughout the country. A handbook of the Association of Indian Universities published in February 2007 lists 281 university institutions. Besides universities of the traditional kind, these include 'deemed universities' such as the Indian Institute of Science at Bangalore and the Tata Institute of Social Sciences at Mumbai, as well as 'institutions of national importance' such as the Indian Institutes of Technology (IITs) and the Indian Statistical Institute.

Apart from there being many more new universities, new kinds of universities, with somewhat more specialized functions than the older

*This is the text of the convocation address delivered at Rabindra Bharati University in 2007.

ones, are now coming up. The earlier universities were built around a core of disciplines in the arts and sciences to which other disciplines were added on. In addition to these, there are now agricultural universities, universities of science and technology, universities of health sciences, law universities, and universities of information technology. Some of those who feel at home in the older type of universities, such as Calcutta and Delhi, find it a little difficult to adjust to the idea of a university of information technology.

Despite the multiplication of universities by a significant factor in the last 60 years, there is a widespread and growing feeling that the opportunities for higher education are still too limited and should be rapidly expanded. Our standards of comparison have changed. A hundred years ago we took the British universities as our standards. Now we look to other countries as well. For their variety, their vitality, and the opportunities they provide, the American universities have become the most attractive in the world. There are now thousands, if not hundreds of thousands, of Indians who study, teach, and do research in the United States. When they return to India, as either visitors or residents, they draw attention pointedly to the contrasts between universities in the two countries. This is partly a result of what has come to be called 'globalization', and we cannot wish it out of existence.

The United States is not the only standard of comparison. There is increasing concern, particularly among our scientists, that China is moving ahead in the field of higher education while we are falling behind. They are expanding at a fast and furious pace, and now count their universities not in the hundreds but in the thousands. At the time of independence we were ahead of the Chinese in the field of higher education. We have expanded our universities but they have expanded theirs faster. How has this reversal come about? What should we do if we are not to fall behind further?

* * *

The demand for the expansion of higher education comes from various quarters, and it is made on various grounds. These grounds may conveniently be grouped together as academic and social. It is said that we need expansion of the universities in order to keep pace with the advance of knowledge and to contribute to that advance. It is also said that we need this expansion in order to create more space in our universities for the various sections of Indian society, particularly for those that have so far had little access to them. These grounds do not appear equally compelling to all those who press for more resources being put into the expansion of universities. Some have their eyes on the number of graduates being produced by the universities; others want to upgrade the facilities for teaching; and yet others are concerned mainly about the amount and quality of research.

The traditional functions of the universities have been the transmission and criticism of existing knowledge and the creation of new knowledge. They were not the only institutions that performed these functions, but from the middle of the nineteenth century onwards, they became the leading ones. In the past, the most important function of the university was the transmission of existing knowledge because new knowledge grew very slowly. This has now changed very substantially and there are scientists and scholars in the universities whose main preoccupation is with the new knowledge that is being continuously created. Some of the ablest among them regard teaching as a burden and a nuisance; yet a university in which nobody teaches can hardly be sustained as an institution.

The growth of knowledge is now so rapid and so extensive that some have begun to say that we are moving into a new type of society which they call 'the knowledge society'. The universities of the twenty-first century, no matter where they are, have to adapt themselves to the requirements of the new type of society that is emerging. Not all individual members of a university, or even all individual universities, can be expected to excel equally in teaching and research, but the university system as a whole must be attentive to the demands of both. If we do not leave enough room for the diversity of talents within a university or among the different universities but try to impose the same requirements on each of them, very little advance will be made in either teaching or research.

The universities have social and not just intellectual obligations; they are both social institutions and centres of learning. Unlike the universities of the past, modern universities aim to be socially inclusive and not exclusive. In India the universities made a good beginning by keeping their doors open to women and members of all castes and communities. But to adopt the principle that admissions and appointments should be made without consideration of caste, community, or gender is one thing, and to accommodate every section of society in sufficient numbers is another. The process of becoming socially fully inclusive in reality and not just in principle has in fact been painfully slow. Here too we have fallen behind not only Europe and the United States but also Japan and China.

There is a natural process of modernization through which universities and other public institutions that were socially exclusive in the beginning gradually become more inclusive. This is largely how the universities in the West changed their social composition from the middle of the nineteenth to the middle of the twentieth century. A similar tendency began to operate in India from the end of the nineteenth century onwards, but its operation was slow and uneven. Women entered the universities but only in very small numbers. Members of disadvantaged castes and communities also entered the universities, but in general they too came in very small numbers. Finally, those who came to the universities, whether as students or as teachers, came very largely from the middle class which until the middle of the twentieth century comprised a very small part of the Indian population.

Indian society was in the past a hierarchical society. Other societies, in Europe and China, were also hierarchical but nowhere else were the principle of hierarchy and the practice of social exclusion carried as far as in India. Dr Ambedkar had said in the Constituent Assembly, 'Democracy in India is only a top-dressing on an Indian soil, which is essentially undemocratic' (1989, vol. 7, p. 38). Beneath the top dressing lay poverty, illiteracy, and untouchability. The Constitution of India rejected the hierarchical principle and put in its place the principle of equality, but the distribution of life chances among castes, communities, and households still remains highly unequal.

The natural process of the transformation of socially exclusive public institutions into socially inclusive ones started early in India but it soon came up against impediments deeply rooted in the structure of Indian society. Other countries that started later have been able to overtake India because the social obstacles to the process of change were less deep-rooted there than in India. But one should not underestimate the resistance to the inclusion of Blacks in the American universities and of women everywhere well into the twentieth century.

* * *

With the adoption of a democratic political order after independence, it became increasingly difficult to support through public funding institutions that remained to a large extent socially exclusive in reality even when in principle they were open to all castes and communities and to women as well as men. Pressures to expand the universities so as to accommodate larger numbers of aspirants began to grow. In all democratic countries, pressures for more places in the universities come mainly from the middle classes and their political spokesmen in the legislatures and the parties. As I have said, in India the middle class was, relative to the total population, very small at the time of independence. It has become much larger and more vociferous in the last 60 years, and hence the pressure for more places in the universities has increased many times.

Equality of opportunity is an important consideration in all democracies, and commitment to it is laid down in the Constitution of India. But what may be guaranteed in principle is not always easy to provide in practice. The disabilities imposed on women and on disadvantaged communities have no doubt been removed. But how far have those abilities that are essential for entry into the higher levels of education been created in India? More and more of those who seek to enter the universities can of course be accommodated by creating more and more seats and posts in them. But if this is done without ensuring that the abilities required for higher education are created more extensively, the inevitable result will be a lowering of the requirements for entry. That in turn will lead to a lowering of the standards of teaching and examining.

Rapid expansion of the universities in response to social and political pressures has led to a relaxation of academic standards in many if not most of them. We are due for a new phase of rapid expansion in the central universities and in the IITs and the Indian Institutes of Management (IIMs). The consequences for teaching and research of the kind of rapid expansion now underway are yet to be seen. When the universities are required to expand rapidly under social and political pressures, the main objective is to increase the number of graduates in all castes and communities. The focus of attention shifts from research to teaching, and from teaching to examining.

Many of our universities have to devote a disproportionate amount of effort to the organization and conduct of examinations. In some of them, the office of the Controller of Examinations is like a fortress. Once the Controller of Examinations at the University of Delhi explained to me why he was against giving too wide a choice of elective or optional courses. He spelt out in great detail the number and variety of question papers that would have to be printed, the complicated examination time-table that would have to be devised, and the number of examiners, tabulators, and moderators that would have to be employed, all with strict attention to confidentiality. I am not sure that I understood all that he said but he certainly managed to make the system appear formidable if not impenetrable.

Controllers have reason to be anxious because the schedule of examinations is persistently upset in many universities. The regularity and routine of teaching too are not always maintained. Universities work on low budgets, and the increase in funding rarely keeps pace with the increase in numbers. Most of the money available to the universities goes into salaries and other establishment charges with very little left for expenditure on libraries and laboratories. The response to social and political pressures on the universities to become more inclusive has generally been to increase the outflow of graduates without adequate attention to the academic worth of the degrees granted to them. It is not surprising that university degrees now stand devalued in the eyes of the wider public.

Research has languished in the universities. Many, if not most, of them have become centres for the transmission of existing knowledge, and that too in a routine and mechanical way, contributing very little to the creation of new knowledge. This was not always true. A single university, the University of Calcutta between the two World Wars, when it was a relatively small place, had such outstanding scientists and scholars as C.V. Raman, Satyendra Nath Bose, Meghnad Saha, Jadunath Sarkar, S. Radhakrishnan, and Suniti Kumar Chatterjee whose research and writing advanced the frontiers of knowledge in their time.

The ablest of our young scientists and scholars no longer find the universities very congenial for research. In the sciences, and to some extent in the social sciences as well, their preference is shifting from the universities to the more compact and specialized research laboratories and institutes, most of which have come up since independence. The movement away from the universities of persons with the ability and aptitude for research will have serious long-term consequences for the academic vitality of the universities. The modern university is based on the principle of the unity of teaching and research. Teaching at the advanced level cannot be adequately done in a place where no research is being conducted. Expansion of the universities is needed, but that expansion should not be allowed to transform the universities into places which do only teaching and examining but where little or no research is done. If the universities fail to create new knowledge or even to keep step with the advance of knowledge, if they use up the intellectual capital accumulated in the past without adding anything to it, they will be failing in their responsibilities to future generations.

* * *

As the middle class expands, the thirst for university degrees and the kind of professional, administrative, and managerial employment for which they are needed will become more widespread. There is no great harm if every year the universities increase the number of persons on whom they confer their degrees. The universities will have to quicken the pace at which they accommodate persons from those classes and communities whose members have so far failed to enter the universities in sufficient numbers. They have to be proactive in identifying and seeking out such persons and encouraging their passage through the system of higher education. But it will be counterproductive if in the process they continue to relax their standards of admissions and appointments. There are some who say that these standards have already been so deeply compromised that it will not matter very much if they are compromised a little further in the interest of a larger social objective. But that is a counsel of despair to which the universities cannot yield.

Maintaining and even advancing academic standards while becoming socially more inclusive is a difficult objective but it is by no means unattainable (see Chapter 4). It cannot be attained unless we understand the problem clearly and face its challenges purposefully. We must continuously keep in sight the distinction between exclusion on social grounds and discrimination on academic grounds. Too many well-meaning persons in public life declare themselves categorically against discrimination as such, without qualification. The universities must not discriminate on grounds of caste, creed, and gender but, rather, adopt measures to act against such discrimination. But can they afford not to discriminate on academic grounds, or on grounds of merit, ability, and performance?

Moving forward with both objectives in sight has proved to be more difficult in India than in other countries. The record of the universities in the West shows that through much of the twentieth century they, in fact, advanced their standards of teaching and research while at the same time becoming socially more inclusive. Why have we had so little success in doing this in India? I have already pointed to the deep and pervasive hold of hierarchical divisions and values in Indian society. A more specific problem is the weak and infirm base of secondary education on which universities have necessarily to depend for the admission of their students.

The different levels of the educational system are closely interlinked although the conditions of access to educational institutions change as we move from one level to another. Unless the schools produce enough students who have been taught sufficiently well to cope with the demands of university education, attempts to make the universities socially more inclusive may appear politically attractive in the short run but will be self-defeating from the academic point of view. Our political managers want large increases in quantity and believe that quality will look after itself; in higher education, quality is of the utmost importance.

In Britain, France, Germany, and other Western countries, the universities expanded throughout the twentieth century, accommodated more persons from disadvantaged classes and communities, and became more and more diverse in their social composition. Today it is easily forgotten that till the end of the nineteenth century the British universities were male preserves and had very little place for children of workers and artisans. This began to change in the twentieth century, and with increasing momentum after World War II. The change was accompanied, if not preceded, by large and substantial changes in the system of secondary education.

Universal elementary education is still to be achieved in India, whereas in one country after another outside India it has become a reality. The distinction between those who had been to school and those who remained unlettered was an important one in Victorian England. It has ceased to be important in Europe, the United States, and Japan, and is ceasing to be important in China. But it remains a stark and palpable division in India.

In those countries in which universal elementary education became established by the middle of the twentieth century, secondary schools of good quality began to extend their reach and gradually became accessible to both boys and girls with ability and initiative from all social classes. Even China now appears to have a large enough population of school leavers who are ready and prepared to take advantage of the increasing number of places becoming rapidly available in the universities. In India, governments want the universities to take in more young men and women from all classes and communities without seriously strengthening or extending the base of secondary education that will qualify students for a meaningful university education.

There are, no doubt, schools in India that provide secondary education that is good enough to qualify their products for university education anywhere. It is no secret that some secondary schools provide better education than is available in many undergraduate colleges. But they are very few in number and expensive and exclusive, and those who come out of them are frustrated and bored by the quality of undergraduate education now generally available even in the metropolitan cities. This is a difficult situation that cannot be remedied simply by putting more pressure on the universities to become socially more inclusive by rapidly expanding their intake of students.

Reference

Constituent Assembly Debates. 1989. *Official Report*, vol. 7. New Delhi: Lok Sabha Secretariat.

Chapter
4

Universities at the Crossroads*

The subject of this chapter is the Indian university and the challenges it faces in the twenty-first century. Discussion and debate on our universities are marked by sharp and growing disagreement between proponents of two different and opposite points of view. There are those who maintain that the universities should be governed solely by pure merit without any consideration of their social composition; they do not generally pause to consider whether merit itself can be defined unequivocally by one single criterion. On the other side are those who maintain that the universities should become fully inclusive socially and give representation to all castes and communities in proportion to their numbers; they have little sympathy for the university's need to discriminate among students and teachers on the basis of their academic ability and performance.

There is a growing feeling that the universities, at least as we have known them up to now, face an uncertain future, not only in India but across the world. That feeling was expressed by many at the symposium on 'The University of the Twenty-First Century' held at the University of Chicago in 1991 to mark its centennial. Professor Edward Shils, the organizer of the symposium, concluded his address to it with the following words: 'Perhaps Napoleon will replace Wilhelm von Humboldt as the guiding star of our academic

*This text was published in *Current Science*, vol. 92, no. 4, 25 February 2007, pp. 441–9.

intellectual life' (1992: 268). Humboldt created the first modern university in Berlin based on the principle of the unity of teaching and research, whereas Napoleon provided the main impetus in France for the *grandes écoles* which were small, compact, and highly selective institutions designed to give expression to the principle of 'careers open to talent'.

A hundred and fifty years ago, even the idea of the university as a popular institution was a new one, not only in India but also in England and in most parts of Europe. The universities were small, selective, and often reclusive places, and they were designed neither to overturn the existing hierarchies nor to produce hundreds of thousands of graduates every year for employment in government and other offices. When the first universities were started in Calcutta, Bombay, and Madras, such a conception of the social responsibility of the university was still in the future.

The universities and their law, medical, and other colleges opened new horizons both intellectually and institutionally in a society that had stood still in a conservative and hierarchical mould for centuries. India had a rich intellectual tradition in disciplines such as mathematics, grammar, logic, and metaphysics, but that tradition had stagnated and atrophied partly because of the narrow and restricted social channels through which it was reproduced and transmitted. The exposure to a new and expanding tradition of learning did a great deal to revive the dormant intellectual energies of Indians, and the universities were in the forefront of this revival.

Furthermore, the universities were among the first open and secular institutions in a society that was governed largely by the rules of kinship, caste, and religion. In that sense they were islands of modernity in a world bound largely by tradition. Right until the time of independence, the universities were few and far between. Their influence did not reach very far or penetrate very deeply into a society that was steeped in poverty, illiteracy, and inequality. But the influence, no matter how restricted, was progressive, both intellectually and institutionally, and this progressive influence appeared to be spreading gradually, though very slowly.

In the last century, the universities did more than any other institution to enlarge the role of women in public life. Their presence in the professions, in administration, in management, in the media, and in other areas of employment in remunerative and responsible positions would not have been possible if the universities and the colleges had not opened their doors to them. Oxford and Cambridge had been in existence for 600 or 700 years before they began to admit women to their degrees. Calcutta University admitted two women to its BA degree in 1883, and they became the first women graduates in the British empire (Basu 2005: 191).

Changes were taking place not only in attitudes towards women but also in attitudes to caste.

If we look at the way in which caste was represented in the period prior to independence, we will find that a large part of the attention was devoted to its ritual aspects, centring around the opposition of purity and pollution. This is what the anthropologist J.H. Hutton (1961: 71–91) called the strictures of caste. The strictures described by Hutton and the majority of anthropologists of his time related to the 'avoidance of pollution through water, food or contact'. The present generation of university students, at least in the metropolitan cities, can scarcely understand what that might mean. If the ritual interdictions of caste now stand largely discredited, at least among the urban middle classes, it is well to remember that the process by which they became discredited first began in the universities and their hostels.

The age-old restrictions of gender and caste did not disappear in the universities, but they came to be questioned there. The education in citizenship also began in the universities. It has been said that in the past, India was a society not of citizens, but of castes and communities. A person's identity, particularly among the Hindus, but to some extent among all religious communities, was defined largely by his caste or sect, and also by his or her gender. Citizenship in our Constitution is an unmediated relationship between the individual and the state without consideration of religion, caste, or sex. The idea of citizenship received a strong impetus from the universities even before the rights of citizenship were laid down in the Constitution.

* * *

The universities had secured a foothold in Indian society as open and secular institutions, and as autonomous centres of study and research when the country entered the era of independence. Their academic achievements were not spectacular, but the pursuit of science and scholarship was taken seriously and regarded as an important and significant value. As institutions, they were not without blemish, but they were relatively free from the more egregious forms of social discrimination that were still pervasive in the wider society. Their influence in society was beneficial, although it did not reach very far.

The prospects for the consolidation and expansion of the universities and their influence seemed good at the time of independence in 1947. India was in advance of most countries outside the West with the possible exception of Japan. It was certainly well ahead of China whose universities did not have the breadth and depth or the self-reliance of the Indian universities in Calcutta, Bombay, Allahabad, and elsewhere. The institutions that had been built in China were severely disrupted by the political turmoil through which the country passed before and after 1949. What survived the turmoil through which the People's Republic of China passed in its early years was almost decimated by the Great Cultural Revolution of 1966 with its anti-intellectualism and its open attack of teachers, scholars, and authors.

Although the two countries entered a new phase of change and development at roughly the same time, India in 1947 and China in 1949, no two persons could have been more different in their attitudes towards the universities than Jawaharlal Nehru and Mao Zedong. The men who wrote the Constitution of India had a very different experience of higher education and a very different orientation to it from the experience and orientation of the men who carried China through war and revolution to the creation of a new republic. There is a streak of chronic anti-intellectualism in India but it did not manifest itself in the Constituent Assembly and remained muted in the early decades of independence.

India was fortunate in having as its first and longest-serving prime minister a person who did not just suffer universities to exist but had a deep and active sympathy for them. It is well known that Nehru loved addressing university gatherings and gave many convocation addresses both in India and abroad. His sympathetic concern for the universities was expressed in a convocation address he delivered in his hometown at the University of Allahabad in the very year of India's independence. That address was an expression of both hope and foreboding. In it he said, 'The universities have much to teach in the modern world and their scope of activity ever enlarges. I am myself a devotee of science and believe the world will ultimately be saved, if it is to be saved, by the method and approach of science'

(Nehru 1958: 329). There was hope that the universities would do well because if they do well, 'then it is well with the nation and the people' (ibid.: 333).

But there was apprehension as well, for 'if the temple of learning itself becomes a home of narrow bigotry and petty objectives, how then will the nation prosper or a people grow in stature?' (ibid). Increasingly, the universities have become battlegrounds for the promotion of every kind of personal and sectional interest. The university is by its nature a place where divergent views are given room for expression. Science and scholarship cannot progress unless divergent views are put to the test of reason and experience. But the disputes that now dominate many if not most of our universities are not over the principles and methods of science and scholarship; they are over pay and promotion and the distribution of seats and posts among different castes, communities, and factions.

Between 1857 and 1947, the universities grew at a slow and leisurely pace. With independence, the tempo of growth became faster. There were barely 30 universities at the time of independence. There are now close to 300 of them. Here I will follow the terminology adopted by the Association of Indian Universities and use the umbrella term 'universities' to cover, in addition to universities pure and simple, what are called 'Deemed to be Universities', such as the Indian Institute of Science and the Tata Institute of Social Sciences, as well as the 'Institutes of National Importance' such as the Indian Statistical Institute and the Indian Institutes of Technology (IITs). Besides there being a larger number of institutions, there is now a greater variety of them.

There are still a few university institutions in which standards of teaching and research are maintained at a fairly high level, but none of the older universities is any longer in the forefront. In an increasing number of them, hardly any research worth the name is done, and even the regularity and routine of ordinary classroom teaching are often dispensed with. In the majority of state universities, virtually the entire budget goes into salaries and other establishment charges, with hardly anything left over for libraries and laboratories. Standards and facilities for undergraduate teaching in many universities are often below what may be found in the better schools in the country.

The growth in the universities in the last 60 years has left most people dissatisfied. There is dissatisfaction with the amount of growth as well as its direction. Many are unhappy that the growth has been slow and limited in extent. They point out that a far smaller proportion of the population is in higher education than in the advanced countries and even China. They would like to see the government put more money into the universities, and many are now talking about exploring other sources of funding for the universities. Others say that the growth in the universities has been unplanned and haphazard, and in response to political pressures. There has been an enormous expansion of knowledge in the last 60 years, but most Indian universities have not even tried to keep pace with it.

* * *

The universities stand at the crossroads today. Especially in India, they are attacked from various quarters. They are no longer seen, as they were in their formative years, as the outposts of a new kind of social and intellectual life in a stagnant and hierarchical society. They are chronically short of funds, but what goes deeper than the shortage of funds is the loss of nerve, the failure of confidence within the university in its own basic purpose and objective.

The universities are attacked for allowing academic standards to decline steadily in a world in which knowledge is expanding rapidly. They are attacked simultaneously for their failure to act in a socially responsible way in the cause of equity and social justice. Much of the attack is indiscriminate and intemperate, but the universities are losing the composure to address even those points of criticism that are reasonable and well judged.

There is growing anxiety, particularly among our scientists, that India is losing its competitive advantage in the field of modern knowledge to China and other countries over which it had such an advantage until recently. If India is to advance or even keep its place as a knowledge society, it will have to invest far more in research and development and in the institutions of higher education. That India needs many more universities and more funds from a diversity of sources is now generally accepted. However, the resources will be wasted if we continue to act in the belief that all universities, the small and the large, the purposeful and the disorderly, the active and the lethargic, should be given the same resources on the assumption that they fulfil more or less the same social need. There is enormous political pressure to build all universities according to the same plan and to have them regulated in the same way by the same external authority. The universities cannot discharge their social and academic responsibilities effectively if those responsibilities are defined by the state and the political parties.

The challenge before our universities in the twenty-first century is to combine two distinct but important objectives. The first objective is to maintain and apply strict standards of academic discrimination, without fear or favour and without consideration of caste, creed, and gender. The second is to make the universities socially more inclusive, in practice and not just in principle. The difficulties of keeping both objectives simultaneously in view are not given the attention they deserve.

Some of our best university institutions still maintain high academic standards and their graduates fit easily into the best universities outside the country and perform very well there. I can speak from personal experience of the Delhi School of Economics, and from hearsay about the Tata Institute of Social Sciences, The Indian Institute of Science, and the IITs and the Indian Institutes of Management (IIMs). But these institutions are not the most inclusive socially in either their faculties or their student bodies. In the eyes of the crusaders for social justice, they are 'elitist', and woe betide any academic institution if it is singled out in Parliament or in a state assembly as being elitist.

There are other institutions that have, as a matter of policy, opened their doors to a much wider cross-section of castes and communities. The southern universities, particularly in Karnataka and Tamil Nadu, have done so since before independence, and such a policy has now come to be adopted by universities in many other parts of the country. The academic record of these universities has not been very encouraging, and there has been a secular trend of decline in their standards of performance. One has only to compare the University of Madras with IIT Madras, or Bangalore University with the National Law School University at Bangalore to appreciate the point I am making.

Is a relaxation in academic standards inevitable as a university becomes more mixed in its social composition? Such a conclusion would be a mistake and contrary to the evidence from many countries, and, indeed, from most parts of India until the early years of independence. In fact, a strong argument can be made that in the long run, universities gain academically and not just socially by becoming more inclusive and by learning to accommodate and manage diversity among their teachers and students. What is decisive is the kind of process through which the principle of social inclusion is translated into practice.

The routes through which sections of society earlier largely excluded from the universities came to be gradually incorporated in them have varied from one case to another. The difference becomes at once evident when we compare the trajectories of inclusion of women with those of the backward castes and communities. Organized political pressure has played little part in the slow but steady inclusion of women in the universities, first as students and shortly afterwards as teachers. Pressure from political parties in both government and opposition has been the main driving force behind the increase in the numbers of students and teachers from the backward castes and communities. In the former case, the accommodation has been achieved without much threat to the autonomy of the university; in the latter it has been at considerable cost to the university's autonomy.

The so-called elite institutions may have failed to admit or appoint many members of the backward castes or communities, but they have accommodated women in increasing numbers. We must not make light of the bias against women that was widespread in academic institutions even when those institutions were formally open to all, irrespective of caste, community, and gender. That bias has not disappeared in India or even in countries with fuller provisions for higher education. But it has been steadily worn down and overcome in the face of the academic achievements of successive generations of women. At first the women in the universities were mainly students and not teachers. But when some of the women students performed brilliantly, it became very difficult to keep them out of faculty positions for very long.

It is now much more widely acknowledged than 50 or 60 years ago that having more women in the universities is good not only for women, but also for the universities. That acknowledgement has been won through much toil and effort and not without many disappointments. It has been a long drawn process and it should lead us to realize that a university may become socially inclusive in more than one way and at more than one step.

There has been since the middle of the nineteenth century a secular trend for universities to move from being 'aristocratic' or socially exclusive to becoming 'popular' or socially inclusive. This trend did not begin at the same time everywhere, and it has not gone the same distance in every country. Even within the same country, the movement, as we have seen, has been uneven. Nevertheless, there is now general recognition of the value that is added to a university when it becomes socially inclusive. In the United States this is referred to as 'diversity', and the social and intellectual value of diversity has now come to be taken for granted. Many American universities, including the best ones, have policies for enhancing their diversity. Such success as these policies have had has been due to the fact that the initiative for them has come mainly from within the university instead of their being imposed on the universities by external political authorities.

It is unrealistic to expect that every public institution, irrespective of its specific tasks and objectives, will, in the natural course of events, come to mirror more or less faithfully all the social divisions in the wider population. It is particularly unwise to seek to arrive at such an outcome through the intervention of the state. Today the advocates for greater representation for the backward classes are no longer satisfied by their gradual incorporation in the universities. They want representation in proportion to population in the interest of equity and social justice, and they want the state to use all the instruments in its hands to bring this about expeditiously.

* * *

Even if we admit that each kind of public institution has its own specific functional requirements, we cannot remain wholly indifferent to its social composition. If the secular trend in the world as a whole is for the universities to become socially more inclusive and diverse, why has this trend ceased to operate or why does it operate so feebly in so many of our universities, and particularly in the ones that enjoy the highest academic standing? In a democratic social and political order, this question has to be addressed seriously in the public interest and in the interest of the universities themselves.

Recognition of the fact that the obstacles to free access operate differently for different institutions and for different sections of society leads to a new set of questions. Access to the most competitive and selective university institutions depends in large measure on how well qualified and prepared the aspirants for admission are. Women from certain classes are now able to enter secondary schools of good quality more easily than are most members of the backward castes.

In Britain until World War II, not many women or children of working class families found their way into the better universities, particularly Oxford and Cambridge, even though there was no formal bar against them. Their entry into them had to await the expansion of secondary education that took place after World War II. What we learn from the experience of the advanced countries of Europe and America is that it is impossible to make the universities socially inclusive in a meaningful and effective way without first creating a broad-based system of secondary schools where education of a reasonably good quality is within the reach of boys and girls from all classes and communities. I am not arguing that any of the countries to which I have just referred has achieved complete success in this regard, but they have travelled much further along that road than we have. It is this that enables their universities to adopt policies for greater social diversity without compromising their academic standards too much.

The main reason why there were few women in the universities in Britain and America before World War II is that few of them had had the benefit of a good secondary education. Even in those countries, education beyond a certain level was not considered necessary or even desirable for women. With changes in attitudes towards women after World War II and the creation of more room for them in secondary schools of good quality, more and more women were academically prepared for entry into the universities and to perform successfully in them. This, rather than any direct intervention by the state, was the main factor behind the increasing presence of women in the universities.

What happened in Britain and other Western countries in the wake of World War II was repeated in some respects in India in the wake of independence. More women started doing well in school and they entered the colleges and universities, where again their achievements came to be acknowledged. At first they did well mainly in the humanities, but soon they entered the departments of science as well as the professional colleges. This change was made possible largely by changes in attitudes and aspirations within the middle-class family, and here some castes and communities were in the forefront while others lagged behind. Government intervention in university admissions and appointments did not play any large part in the process.

When we look back at the incorporation of women into the universities, whether in the West or in India, we see that what stood against their fuller incorporation was the social bias against their education rather than any lack of innate ability. While such bias was undoubtedly present inside the universities, its deeper roots lay in the family and the community. Till the time of independence, it was not considered proper in many, if not most, Indian families for mature girls to enter institutions where their fellow students and their teachers would be mostly men. Having separate institutions for women solved the problem to some extent but it was not a satisfactory solution for postgraduate study and research. It was only when women were allowed to move more freely on their own that they made their way more fully into the universities, and their successful performance there led to a further easing of the bias against them.

It should be pointed out at once that the women who are entering the best university institutions in increasing numbers do not come equally from all castes and classes. They belong mainly to the upper castes and the middle class. While caste is undoubtedly important in determining life chances, the divisions of class based on income, wealth, and occupation are no less important. Women from the middle and upper-middle classes in the metropolitan cities have better chances than all other women. The pressure of early marriage is weakest among them. Good, though expensive, schools are available in metropolitan cities, and middle-class families are increasingly willing to send their daughters to the best ones, which are often co-educational, which prepare them for admission not only to the most competitive arts and science colleges, but also to the professional ones.

The situation for women, irrespective of caste or community, in villages and small towns is very different. There the pressure on the girl to marry by the time she is 18, and even before, is strong. Good schools are not within easy reach, especially for girls; and the limited resources of the family are used for creating opportunities for sons rather than daughters.

* * *

Having shown that the social obstacles to the larger presence of women in the universities are to be found more outside than within the universities, I now turn to the complex and controversial subject of caste. Before turning to the specifics of the Indian case, I may point out that it will be unrealistic to expect all universities—the good, the bad, and the indifferent—to incorporate persons from every section of society in proportion to their strength in the population. Such an outcome has not been achieved by any university system anywhere in the world, and it is unlikely to be ever achieved in the future.

It still remains true that there are many castes and communities, including some that are quite populous, whose presence in the more select universities is so small as to be a scandal. There is no reason to believe that the distribution of individual ability has anything to do with the social division into castes and communities. The implication of this unusual pattern of distribution is that a vast pool of talent lies undetected, unrecognized, and unprepared for admission into the better university institutions. The responsibility for this does not lie with the universities alone; it lies as much, if not more, with a whole range of institutions, from the family to the school, for failing to play their part in identifying and preparing the individuals concerned for entry into the best universities and performing successfully in them.

The comparison with China is particularly relevant. Both societies were hierarchically organized in the past, although hierarchical values were more deeply entrenched in India than in China. India and China were both beginning to set up modern universities by the end of the nineteenth century. In both countries the universities were small in size and few in number. India had the advantage over China in having started a little earlier and attained higher standards of academic performance. There is no reason to believe that in the early decades of the twentieth century the Indian universities were the more 'aristocratic' and the Chinese ones the more 'popular'.

The Chinese system of higher education underwent a great upheaval during the Cultural Revolution of 1966–76. One of the principal objectives of the Cultural Revolution was to dismantle the elitism that had survived in the Chinese university system. The movement under Mao provides the most spectacular example in history of the ruthless attack on elitism in the universities in the pursuit of a political agenda that had no concern for science and scholarship. The attack on elitism has become a routine with certain populist movements in India, but such movements have nothing of the mobilizing power or the destructive energy of the Cultural Revolution in the last decade of Mao's regime.

The Chinese universities have been given a new lease of life in the last two decades mainly as a result of the remarkable turnaround in China's economic policy. Under Deng, the main thrust of the policy was to attain high and sustained rates of economic growth through rapid industrialization. This has called for a very different kind of policy for higher education from the policy of levelling under Mao. The universities have been steered away from the compulsions of populism to meet the need for creating superior, if not elite, institutions that can compete with the best of their kind in the world. Having burnt their fingers with the Cultural Revolution, the Chinese authorities are very careful to keep their best university institutions away from populist pressures.

Chinese society, as a whole, has in the last seven or eight decades undergone a process of upheaval and churning that has had no parallel in India. Radical movements in India have at best attacked political institutions and structures. They have not attacked, as the Chinese did relentlessly, the basic institutions of family, marriage, and kinship. It has long been accepted that the family system was the basic and fundamental institution of Chinese society (Hsu 1948; Freedman 1966). The continuous attack on it over several generations has shaken up and loosened China's traditional system of stratification. Women have acquired freedom of movement and of opportunity much more extensively than in India. The social standing due to birth in a particular family or lineage counts for much less than it did in the past. In India, that standing no longer has any legal recognition; but it still has wide social recognition.

India has undergone some social churning, but its effects have not spread very widely or gone very deep. To be sure, political conflicts of one kind or another have been endemic, and the university campus has been a battleground for rival parties, rival factions, and rival castes and communities. These endemic rivalries and hostilities have been a major depressant of academic performance, but it is doubtful how far they have contributed to the restructuring of economic disparities or the circulation of persons from various social classes across the different levels of the hierarchy.

Where the universities have become socially more inclusive by a change in their caste composition, this has happened less through the free and unimpeded circulation of individuals across the educational and occupational systems than through the adoption of quotas in both admissions and appointments for the different castes and communities.

Many advocates of caste quotas concede that they are only a second-best solution, but they add that in India quotas are the only solution that can work. This argument has been so widely and persistently presented that it requires to be seriously addressed.

While bias and prejudice undoubtedly exist in Indian society, their presence is by no means unique to it. Social prejudice based on gender, race, religion, ethnicity, or caste exists in one form or another in most if not all societies. There is at best a difference of degree between India and other countries. It is difficult to agree that the very limited presence of the backward castes in the best university institutions is due solely to the social bias against them. Why has the bias against them remained unchanged or, as some say, even increased when the bias against women in those very institutions has declined significantly? The trajectories by which women have found their way into the elite universities in India are remarkably similar to the trajectories followed by women in the advanced industrial societies. Why have the trajectories of the backward castes been so different?

No doubt, caste is different from gender, and caste bias operates somewhat differently from gender bias. But the evidence does not suggest that caste bias on the university campus was from the start stronger than gender bias, or that the decline of gender bias, which has undoubtedly taken place, was a smooth and easy process, in India or anywhere else.

It will be very difficult to maintain that in Indian society as a whole, caste prejudice has remained unaltered in the last 50–60 years. Strong caste prejudice against the Dalits continues to exist in many but not all parts of the country. Social prejudice against castes belonging to the middle levels of the hierarchy has declined in many respects to a greater extent than social prejudice against women. Again, this is not to say that prejudice of either kind has disappeared.

As I have said earlier, the ritual restrictions of caste have dwindled. The association between caste and occupation has loosened, and the rules of caste endogamy have also become weaker. Where then does the caste bias that continues to exist at the beginning of the twenty-first century draw its sustenance from? If caste has acquired a new lease of life in independent India, it is mainly through organized politics. When M.N. Srinivas (1962: 15–41) stated in a presidential address to the Indian Science Congress nearly 50 years ago that caste was acquiring a new lease of life, many found the statement more surprising than convincing. But Srinivas had chosen his examples carefully, and all of them came from the domain of politics. The use of caste for mobilizing political support has come to be accepted as a commonplace to the point that many now believe that caste bias is inextinguishable.

There were great variations in the extent to which caste consciousness prevailed in the universities at the time the country became independent. The universities of Madras and Mysore (set up in 1857 and 1916, respectively) may be contrasted with those of Calcutta (set up in the same year as the University of Madras) and Delhi (set up six years after the University of Mysore). I can speak from personal experience of Calcutta, where I was a student in 1950–7, and Delhi, where I have taught since 1959; in neither of the two was caste a subject of much interest in the early decades of independence, except among specialists in sociology. It was very different in the southern universities. In Delhi, if one wanted to know about the role of caste in education and employment, one asked the sociologists—or one's colleagues from south India.

Caste consciousness on the campus grew with the spread in the demand for caste quotas to regions where such demands had been absent or weak in the past. The agitations over the recommendations of the Mandal Commission in 1990 brought caste consciousness into many universities that had been relatively free from it in the early decades of independence. To be sure, caste was used for the mobilization of political support even then; as I have said, Srinivas pointed this out in his address of 1957. But the use of caste in politics then was justified on pragmatic and not ideological grounds. The grounds shifted after 1977 when support for caste quotas and, more generally, the use of caste in politics began to be justified ideologically by the appeal to equality and social justice. This brought in its wake a new kind of politics for which the term 'identity politics' is generally used.

As I have already pointed out, caste is not just a form of organization; it is as much a form of consciousness. It is true that the consciousness alone cannot create social divisions out of nothing. But it can bring into the open divisions that were submerged; sharpen cleavages that were growing faint; and give a clearer focus to practices that were diffuse. If caste has dug its roots deeper into the universities today, the main responsibility for that lies in the way in which politics has come to be organized. Political parties, across a wide ideological spectrum, including the two communist parties, have thrown their weight in favour of caste quotas. No party can today openly oppose quotas for fear of its vote banks turning against it. We now have a very different political climate from the climate of 50 years ago.

* * *

Caste quotas in education and employment have caught the public imagination because they draw attention to an unresolved problem. The uneven distribution of castes and communities in university institutions is not just a matter of statistics, it is a social fact. Disparities have declined to some extent, but in the most competitive and coveted institutions they have not declined sufficiently to the satisfaction of all.

There is general agreement that equality of opportunity is a desirable objective, and commitment to it is written into the Constitution of India. Equality of opportunity depends not just on the removal of disabilities but also on the creation of abilities. Access to universities is restricted because of the insufficient and uneven development of secondary education. However, except for the Scheduled Castes and Scheduled Tribes, successful completion of secondary education is frustrated more by low household income than by low status in the hierarchy of caste (Sundaram 2006). Caste is important, but, at least in the context of higher education, class is no less important. What is attributed to caste bias can often be more easily explained by disparities in material resources. We must not, in the heat generated by identity politics, lose sight of the fact that disparities of wealth, income, and occupation act independently of caste, and act in important ways, on the distribution of life chances among individuals.

The Indian middle class is now quite large and it is no longer made up of persons from only a few top castes. There is a growing middle class among the intermediate castes which comprise the core of the Other Backward Classes, and this section of the Other Backward Classes is hungry for more and better quality education for its children, and especially its sons. Its leading members, many of whom are prominent in public life, are not satisfied today with just any kind of higher education for their children; they want places in the best university institutions for them. There they have to contend with children from equally well-to-do upper caste families who have had an earlier start in the race for the limited facilities available for the best kind of higher education. When the latecomers are unable to cope with the competition, they demand that places be reserved for them in the interest of equity and justice.

We are left in the end with two questions. First, does social policy have any part to play in making the universities socially more inclusive and ensuring greater diversity on the campus? Second, is a policy of numerical quotas for castes in proportion to their population the best policy for the purpose?

Caste quotas in education and employment have been in operation in one form or another for more than 80 years. Their consequences have been mixed at best. Where they have been used on a massive scale, they have contributed to a better mix of castes and communities, but they have also contributed to a steady decline in academic standards. Their contribution to a better mix of castes and communities is self-evident; their contribution to a decline in academic standards is not equally evident because other factors, not directly related to caste, have also contributed to the decline.

The British first introduced quotas in education and employment in the erstwhile state of Mysore and in Madras Presidency more than 80 years ago. But they were introduced on a small scale, and as a matter of policy and not of right. Since then the scale of caste quotas has increased enormously and most political parties treat them as matters of right and not of policy. These two features in combination have virtually closed the door to all policies other than the policy of numerical quotas to make the universities more socially inclusive and more diverse.

There are many today who are worried about the lack of diversity in the best universities and the very limited presence in them of members of the intermediate and the lower castes, but they have grave misgivings about the damage to academic standards that is being done by the reckless expansion of caste quotas. Unfortunately, they have given little serious thought to alternatives to numerical quotas for enhancing the diversity of the better universities and making them socially more inclusive. It may not be too late even now to address the problem in a purposive and determined way.

Affirmative action in the universities seeks to create special opportunities for members of socially disadvantaged groups over and above the equal opportunities available to all, while maintaining a close watch on the effects of the policy on academic standards. Such a policy was adopted in the United States roughly 40 years ago, and although it has lost favour in recent years, it still has advocates among serious American academics (Dworkin 2003). The great advantage of the American approach was its flexibility and its decentralized character. Although the US courts have become increasingly critical of the programme, there is every reason to believe that such a programme, with suitable modifications, will be strongly endorsed by the Indian courts.

The defining feature of the kind of affirmative action that I have in mind is that it is based on a respect for the autonomy of institutions and on trust in their selection procedures. The two aspects are closely related. The grant of autonomy is predicated on a degree of trust in the university's capacity to administer its selection procedures without fear or favour and in a socially responsible way. Where universities are deprived of their autonomy for lack of trust in their admissions and appointments practices, academic standards are bound to fall, if not immediately, then in the long run.

In the system of affirmative action I have in mind, admissions and appointments committees are encouraged and trusted to act in a socially responsible manner so as to make the university a more inclusive and a more diverse institution in the long run. Other things being equal, a committee will be expected to prefer the candidate from the disadvantaged community over the general candidate. Other things being a little less than equal, the preference could still be for the socially disadvantaged candidate. How far the committee will go in accommodating candidates from disadvantaged groups will be left to its academic judgement within a broad framework of preferences determined in the university and not outside it. What is crucial is the freedom to exercise academic judgement in the relaxation of standards to meet an agreed social objective.

When committees are given the freedom to act according to their own judgement, they will not all act to produce identically the same outcome everywhere. Some will be more accommodating in the interest of diversity and others more stringent in the interest of academic excellence. Academic committees rarely start from a position of full agreement among all members before reaching a decision. There will also be variation between different committees, different faculties, and different universities. Uniformity and standardization are bureaucratic and not academic virtues.

As I have said, it is widely maintained that no form of affirmative action other than strict numerical quotas can work in India. This argument has been repeated for so long that it has become the common sense of most educated Indians. This common sense has never been put to any serious test in India through programmes for affirmative action of the kind that have worked in other countries, including the United States.

Numerical quotas have worked well from the viewpoint of social inclusion, but badly from that of academic discrimination. They have tilted the balance away from academic to social and political considerations. Their application on a large and expanding scale has enlarged the powers of the bureaucracy over the university faculty. The selection process is monitored from outside to ensure compliance with quotas that are themselves determined by the government. The bureaucracy cracks the whip over the university and demands explanations for shortfalls in the quotas. This development has over the years robbed admissions and appointments committees of much of their initiative and undermined their self-confidence.

The problem with quotas is not simply that they have made short work of intelligence, but that in the long run they have acted as a serious depressant on effort. Few will deny that the level of effort among both students and teachers has gone down in our universities. Caste quotas alone cannot be held responsible for this, but they have been an important contributory factor. Beneficiaries of caste quotas have come to believe that their entry into the university of their choice and their passage through it is a vindication of a social claim that cannot be set aside on merely academic grounds. They have been encouraged in this belief by powerful political forces outside the universities, and many within the universities have increasingly yielded to it.

Those within the universities who care seriously for science and scholarship are demoralized by the devaluation of 'merit', which has come to be used as a shorthand for a whole gamut of attributes such as intelligence, talent, ability, effort, and perseverance. Advance in science and scholarship cannot take place without the recognition and reward of individual achievement, and the universities are being left with less and less room to provide such recognition and reward.

Universities have obligations not only as centres of learning but also as social institutions. Those obligations are of a somewhat different kind in a democratic society from what they might have been in a hierarchical one. Our better universities have not been sufficiently mindful of the value that is added in the long run, academically and not just socially, by their enhancing their diversity and becoming socially more inclusive. They have not been proactive, as the better American universities have been, in making themselves socially more inclusive and diverse. They have only reacted, usually resentfully, to dictates from the government to meet quotas in admissions and appointments, usually determined through political bargains. The ideal of the university as an ivory tower is an anachronism in the twenty-first century. If the universities value their autonomy and want to protect it, they must show more initiative in devising and adopting policies that will change their social composition in the long run and make them more diverse and socially more inclusive. That it is possible to do this without seriously compromising academic standards has been shown over and over again by universities in other countries.

References

Basu, Aparna. 2005. 'A Century and a Half's Journey: Women's Education in India, 1850s to 2000', in Bharati Ray (ed.), *Women of India*, New Delhi: Sage Publications.

Dworkin, Ronald. 2003. 'The Court and the Universities', *The New York Review of Books*, vol. L, no. 8, pp. 8–11.

Freedman, M. 1966. *Chinese Lineage and Society*. London: Athlone Press.

Hsu, Francis L.K. 1948. *Under the Ancestor's Shadow*. London: Routledge & Kegan Paul.

Hutton, J.H. 1961. *Caste in India*. New Delhi: Oxford University Press.

Nehru, Jawaharlal. 1958. *Speeches: 1946–49*, vol. 1. New Delhi: Government of India.

Shils, Edward. 1992. 'The Service of Society and the Advancement of Learning in the Twenty-First Century', *Minerva*, vol. XXX, no. 2, pp. 242–68.

Srinivas, M.N. 1962. *Caste in Modern India and Other Essays*. Bombay: Asia Publishing House.

Sundaram, K. 2006. 'On Backwardness and Fair Access to Higher Education in India: Some Results from NSS 55th Round Surveys 1999–2000'. Delhi: Delhi School of Economics (unpublished manuscript).

Chapter 5

The School and the Community*

Indian society is still a highly stratified society in which the channels of individual mobility are narrow and restricted. In the modern world, this state of affairs is unhealthy from the economic as well as the political point of view, but it cannot be remedied without massive advances in education in both quantitative and qualitative terms. Elementary education must not only be made available to all, but its standard must be such that those who receive it are able to put it to some use in subsequent phases of their lives.

It is well to remember that the idea that all children, irrespective of class, community, and gender, should go to school and spend a minimum period of time in it is a relatively new one, not only in India but in the world as a whole. Even in countries such as England, France, and Germany, children of peasants and workers did not all go to school as recently as in the nineteenth century. One has only to read the novels of Dickens, Balzac, and Tolstoy to realize how important socially, economically, and politically the division was between the lettered and the unlettered. Effective participation of all members of society in civic and political life had to await the effacement of that division.

Universal elementary education does not do away with all inequalities, but it does undermine some of the most odious forms

*This text was published in the *Journal of Educational Planning and Administration*, vol. XXI, no. 3, July 2007, pp. 191–201.

of social exclusion. While social stratification continues to exist in Britain, France, Germany, and other Western countries, the social and political significance of class divisions has been reduced through increased individual mobility across households and across communities. Inequalities in the distribution of life chances are a reality, but so are high rates of individual mobility. Universal elementary education is not a sufficient condition for the changes experienced by the advanced countries in the last hundred years, but it is a necessary condition for them. Without education, for which elementary education provides the base, the chances of individual mobility in a class-divided society are severely limited.

This essential condition for a society to take its place in the modern world remains unfulfilled in India even 60 years after independence. The continuing divide between those who enjoy the benefits of education and those who have little or no access to it is perhaps the most significant index of the backwardness of a nation in the twenty-first century. As I have just pointed out, that divide was common in many if not most countries of the world till the end of the nineteenth century. But other countries, including Japan and China, have moved ahead at an increasing pace whereas we have just managed to crawl along.

There are many factors responsible for our failure in the field of elementary education. Hierarchical values and attitudes have been more deeply entrenched and prevailed over a longer span of time in India than in any other country in the world. These values and attitudes have been particularly marked in the cultivation of learning which was made the exclusive preserve of a small number of communities. It was not simply a matter of there being not enough schools but of a rooted belief that learning from books was meant only for a few and not for all. The conviction about their own superior aptitude of the few at the top was matched by the apathy and fatalism of the masses of people. Neither the sense of inborn superiority nor the apathy and fatalism have fully disappeared.

The hierarchical attitudes of the upper castes were carried over into the new middle class that began to emerge from the end of the nineteenth century. It was that class which was, and still is, responsible for the development of education in the country. While it paid lip service to the principle of equality, it created and administered institutions for the education of its own children, leaving to their fate the vast masses of children from the submerged strata of society.

The schools in the rural areas and even in the towns and cities were few and far between, and they were generally of poor and indifferent quality. The indifferent quality of such schools reinforced the apathy towards education of the disadvantaged classes and communities.

Despite the disappointingly slow pace of change, things have not stood still in the last 60 years. There have indeed been developments in the field of education, but those developments have been highly uneven. Literacy rates have risen, and, even though patches of illiteracy still remain, there is good reason to believe that those patches will continue to shrink. New schools are being established and additional provisions are being made for their funding.

It is well to remember that the provision of free and compulsory education for all children up to the age of 14 years was made a Directive Principle of State Policy in the Constitution of India in 1950. More recently, primary education has been made into a fundamental right. This was done in response to the widespread expression of public concern over the poor state of education in the country. How far making what was a matter of policy into a matter of right will by itself change the horizon of opportunities and expectations is difficult to foretell. But there is undoubtedly greater awareness all around of the benefits of education and the need to make those benefits available to all, irrespective of class, community, and gender.

We are still in the early stages of building a secure and dependable system of universal elementary education in India. By a secure and dependable system of education I mean one that is attentive not only to the numbers of school entrants and school leavers but also pays attention to the kind of education the schools are able to provide. There is no doubt that the number of children in school is increasing and the financial outlay on elementary education is also rising. On the other hand, our knowledge of how elementary schools actually work in different social settings is both very sketchy and very patchy. I will later stress, at an appropriate place, the need to undertake more research, on a sustained basis, on the ways in which schools of different kind operate as social institutions.

Going just by numbers in matters relating to education, particularly in a society as highly differentiated and stratified as ours, can be deceptive and misleading. Indian society is divided into many classes and communities, and it will be unrealistic to presume that those divisions will not cast their shadows on the schools where elementary education is provided. There are elementary schools in the metropolitan cities to which the educated professional classes send their children with a strong sense of how well they can prepare them for their passage through secondary and higher education. Other schools are poorly or very poorly endowed with teachers who are ill-trained and frequently absent, and where very little teaching is done. There is no country in the world where there are no disparities among elementary schools, but such disparities take their most extreme form in India. In the broadest sense, stratification among schools reflects stratification in the wider society.

Education does not eliminate social inequality. It has not done so in any country, and it will be unrealistic to expect it to do so in India in the near or even the distant future. But it can and should eliminate the more extreme forms of it and reduce its rigours by enlarging the possibilities of individual mobility. A society that encourages and promotes individual mobility is not a society that has done away with social stratification, but it is closer to the ideals of democracy than one which is both hierarchical and resistant to individual mobility.

* * *

Modern education has a certain formal organization that cannot be wished away, no matter how greatly we deplore its excesses. A certain degree of formal organization became inescapable as the demand for education became more widespread, not to say universal. In the past and until quite recently, only a few went to school while the rest received such education as they could from the home or the community or some other agency. It cannot be too strongly emphasized that the idea that every person should spend some part of his or her life in an educational institution is a modern one. Now, what is true of every institution is that, while it provides certain facilities, it also imposes certain constraints, and the school as an institution is no exception to this rule.

As education became more institutionalized, it also became more rule bound. Such rules may be more rigid or more flexible, but in every case they must correspond to the aims and objectives of the institutions they seek to govern. It would be unreasonable to regulate a primary school by rules that may be appropriate to a secondary school, just as it would be inappropriate to regulate a university by rules for regulating the conduct of both teachers and students in a secondary school. The conditions of access to a primary school cannot be the same as those to a university. Those who point to the linkages between primary, secondary, and higher education sometimes overlook the obvious fact that different educational institutions are entrusted with different tasks and, hence, they cannot all be regulated by a single set of rules.

In the modern world, primary education is the point of entry into a vast and complex institutional system that has many grades and levels. It will be generally agreed that primary education should be available to all, and that every child, boy or girl, should find a place in a primary school. I must repeat that this is a modern viewpoint that has made its way into the world only since the middle or even the end of the nineteenth century. Even at the time of independence, the majority of children in the relevant age group were out of school in India. We have made some progress since then but, given our material and intellectual resources, that progress leaves much to be desired.

We adopted the principle of universal elementary education at the time of independence and wrote it into the Constitution of India. As I have already noted, it is now not just a matter of policy but also a matter of right. Making admission to primary school universal means that there should be no discrimination in the matter of admission on the basis of caste, creed, or gender, or on the basis of ability or performance. It is generally acknowledged that tests of scholastic aptitude are inappropriate and should be dispensed with in admissions to the first level of the educational system, although such tests cannot be avoided for admission to a college or a university.

Although the principle of universal elementary education was adopted at the time of independence, there were not enough schools in the country at that time to which all children could be admitted. This was true not only of the remote rural areas but also of many towns and cities. I do not wish to go into the story of our failure to build new schools on the scale required in the early years of independence. We left too much in the hands of the government, and the government did not do enough.

There has been a considerable increase in the number of elementary schools in the last couple of decades although there are not enough of them even now to provide for all. The increase in the number of schools has been accompanied by a differentiation of quality and standard. Official statistics dwell on the increase in numbers as, indeed, they should; they tell us very little about variations in what is taught and how it is taught even at the point of entry into the educational system. Yet, a close examination of these variations is indispensable if we are to understand how disparities in ability and performance increase and intensify as students move upwards from one stage to the next in the educational system. Those whose education in elementary school has been deficient fare badly at higher levels of education where tests of ability and performance are indispensable. It is wrong to expect those who have been taught poorly, or not at all, in elementary school to perform adequately in tests of admission to the university, and then to attribute their failure to the social prejudices of the professors.

Differentiation and stratification within the educational system are features of all large and complex modern societies. We know a great deal about the ways in which they operate in countries such as England, France, and the United States (Boudon 1974; Jencks et al. 1979; Devine 2004), but very little about their actual operation in India. One can say on the basis of a general understanding of human societies that they are likely to be more extreme in India than elsewhere. Ours is a highly stratified society marked by extremes of inequality in the distribution of life chances among individuals and households. It will be unrealistic to expect that educational institutions in India can be insulated from the inequalities that permeate the rest of society.

I would like to emphasize that differentiation and stratification in education are present at the very point of entry into the system, at the level of the primary school itself. Educated parents have become increasingly conscious of the need to monitor the school work of their children so that their passage through the successive levels of the system is smooth and easy. Educators may inveigle against applying pressure for scholastic achievement at such an early age, but middle-class parents often have other ideas for their children. In an increasing number of urban middle-class homes, the grooming for scholastic success begins even before admission to primary school.

There is now a large and expanding middle class not only in the major metropolitan cities but also in the smaller cities and towns. There was a middle class even 60 years ago, but it was relatively small and its expansion slow. Things have changed substantially in the last couple of decades. A defining feature of the middle class today is its keen appreciation of the opportunities for upward mobility. It wants advancement for itself through education and professional employment, and it will pay any price to secure that advancement for its children. Anyone who has had anything to do with education will know what members of the emerging middle class are prepared to do to secure admission in a good school for their children right at the point of entry.

Until the time of independence there was less anxiety among parents over the education of their children, and it was confined to a small section of the middle class whose members belonged mainly to a handful of upper castes. Today, the education of children with a view to planning their future careers has become a concern with growing numbers of manual workers in the organized sector. Large public sector undertakings have schools for the children of their employees, and these schools act as important channels of upward mobility. Those who work in offices and factories want not only schools but good schools for their offspring. If a manual worker happens to work in the Bhilai Steel Plant or with a company belonging to the Reliance Group, he may be able to secure better schooling for his children than a clerk or even a school teacher in a provincial town.

Not all manual workers are employed in the organized sector. In fact, the majority of them work outside that sector. There the prospects for the schooling of children are very different. For the vast masses of migrant workers and other workers in casual employment, living from hand to mouth and moving from one job to another, education in a good school or, for that matter, in any sort of school is not within easy reach. They lack not only the material resources but even the information and the aspiration that are spreading across all levels of the middle class and into the organized working class.

When we look at schooling in India today, we encounter a whole range of situations, corresponding to differences in resources, in perceptions, and in aspirations. These differences are not random, but structured hierarchically. They correspond to unequal life chances among parents and generate unequal life chances for their children. Such differences and inequalities in life chances among parents are not unknown elsewhere but they are particularly conspicuous in India.

There has been an increase in public concern over elementary education in the last 10 or 15 years. There is greater awareness of the price being paid for past neglect and gathering enthusiasm for doing what was not done in the early phase of independence. My sense is that the enthusiasm is driven by a certain measure of wishful thinking about what can be done to establish equality of opportunity in elementary education here and now, and in secondary and higher education in the short run. Our plans and projects are unlikely to bear fruit if we wish out of existence the reality and obduracy of social divisions in India and in particular the divisions of class based on wealth, employment, occupation, income, and education.

* * *

How we address issues of social policy depends in some measure on how we look at social reality. There are two contrastive perspectives on society that are commonly encountered in our country. The first I will refer to as the 'fatalistic' and the second as the 'utopian' perspective. The fatalistic perspective is based on the presumption that things are as they are because that is how they have always been and that is how they will continue to be; the utopian perspective, on the other hand, presumes that any desirable state of affairs can be brought into being provided people with the necessary good will are prepared to bring it into being.

The utopian and the fatalistic orientations are not characteristic of two distinct and separate sets of persons. They are often found in alternate phases in one and the same individual. Where the utopian expectations are extravagant and unrealizable, they are likely to be frustrated and followed by a fatalistic turn of mind. In that sense there is a kind of natural affinity between the utopian and the fatalistic dispositions. In contrast with the fatalistic or the utopian orientation is the pragmatic orientation which does not accept the existing reality as unchangeable, but also does not pursue programmes of change that wish the constraints of the real world out of existence.

The idea that a school system can be designed in such a way that every school will have material, pedagogical, and other resources to provide education of the same quality and standard to everyone is not a workable one from the policy point of view in a country like India. A school system, if it is properly designed, can do something to reduce the inequalities of life chances among persons. It cannot dismantle at one stroke—or even through a succession of Five-Year Plans—all the accumulated inequalities of a hierarchical society with which people have lived more or less comfortably for 2,000 years.

It may be useful to consider very briefly what it takes to dismantle the entire structure of inequality in education and society. The Chinese example has some useful lessons for us. During the Great Proletarian Cultural Revolution of 1966–76, the Chinese did succeed to a large extent in dismantling the established hierarchies in education, but the success was achieved only by paying an enormous price in social dislocation and human suffering. Indians who look forward to the kind of revolutionary transformation the Chinese underwent do not ponder sufficiently on the costs that it entailed. And inequalities in the Chinese educational system did not disappear but only went underground to come out into the open once again.

Education can and should be put to the service of creating a better society, but our approach should be realistic. It undoubtedly contributes to the removal of many odious distinctions and it also creates channels for individual mobility (Erikson and Goldthorpe 1993). But education also contributes to the reproduction of inequality, and that fact must not be lost to sight (Bourdieu and Passeron 1977). A great deal depends on the structure of the society and the political environment within which the educational system operates.

The first and most urgent priority should be to put every child of the appropriate age into elementary school and to provide for a sufficient number of elementary schools that will have the basic material, social, and cultural resources required for decent education. This can be done without agonizing about the quality and standard of elementary education that rich and resourceful middle-class parents driven by the ambition for upward mobility are able to buy for their own children.

We are too easily diverted by the rhetoric of equality from solvable practical problems. Here I would like to make a distinction between equality and universality, and make a strong case for the latter. Universality requires that certain basic facilities and capabilities be placed within the reach of every member of society without consideration of individual merit or need; in short, that they be made universally available. Obvious examples of what can and should be made universally available are primary education and primary health care.

The educational system will generate its own inequalities in due course of time. We may succeed in regulating those inequalities up to a point, but we cannot eradicate them. This is particularly true in a world in which knowledge is advancing at an explosive rate. Even if we succeed in creating equality of opportunity in the school, the college, or the university, we will fail to have equality of outcome. If we strive to maintain uniformity of outcome, we will only succeed in stifling effort, initiative, and the pursuit of excellence. All we can aim to do is to see that social advantage does not translate too easily into scholastic advantage, and that is by no means an easy thing to do.

There is no educational system that is not embedded in a social system. In a society such as ours it is inevitable that different schools will be endowed with different, not to say unequal, material and pedagogic resources. It is the obligation of the state and other public bodies to see that no school falls below a certain level, to aid and support those that have fallen behind, and not pull back those that are moving ahead. The philosophy of the Levellers is not a good philosophy on which to build an educational system.

* * *

It will be agreed by all that we need to provide elementary education for all, that our record in this respect has been rather poor so far, and that we must do a great deal more to catch up with the rest of the world. But who is to take the responsibility for doing what needs to be done, that schools meeting the basic minimum requirements of pedagogy are created and maintained? It is not simply a matter of putting more money into education, it is also a matter of creating functioning institutions in which teaching and learning can take place. The government can provide the funds, and the bureaucracy can see that the funds are properly accounted for. But can the government and its bureaucracy create and maintain the institutions that are indispensable for teaching and learning? I am not speaking now of good or bad schools from a scholastic point of view, but of the regularity and routine of the everyday activities which are essential to the life of the school as an institution.

I cannot say much from personal knowledge or experience of the health of our elementary schools as institutions in which regular activities are performed according to the clock and the calendar. There will obviously be a great deal of variation across schools in different locations in the different parts of the country. But even where the problems of funding have been attended to, we cannot take the institutional health of the school for granted. What little experience I have had of higher education has made me realize that the institutional life of the college or the university is often very sluggish or even moribund. In many such places very little goes on. Attendance is irregular; classes are not held according to the time table; examinations are delayed or disrupted; and there is a general atmosphere of apathy and indifference among both students and teachers.

We know next to nothing about the social atmosphere in different types of elementary schools, whether it is marked by good cheer, apathy, or sheer neglect all around. Does the school appear to its pupils as something to be enjoyed or merely endured? The statistics of teacher absenteeism provide little comfort although, here again, there are bound to be very large variations between schools of different types. Statistics do not, in any case, tell the whole story. Teachers may mark themselves present but actually do little for the care of those put in their charge. I am told that there are many schools, now even in the villages, where teachers do most of their teaching outside the school as private tutors or coaches for additional payment.

What the state and its agencies cannot be expected to do in terms of social participation or regulation can legitimately be expected of the community. Indeed, it is difficult to see how an effective system of elementary schools can be established and maintained without some involvement from the local community. Wherever elementary schools have worked well, they have done so because of the support of the community.

There has been a waxing of enthusiasm for the community in recent years, partly in response to the disenchantment with the state and its agencies. I do not wish to throw cold water on this enthusiasm, but we need to take a hard look at what we call the community in India. It may turn out that, instead of being the perfect solution, the community is part of the problem. Many well-informed and knowledgeable persons, who are fully aware of the deep divisions and inequalities—of class, of caste, and of gender—in Indian society as a whole, somehow manage to persuade themselves that the Indian community is free from those divisions and inequalities. This utopian vision of the community does not fit the actual reality of the Indian village very well.

Many of the leaders of the nationalist movement represented the Indian village as a 'little republic' and a haven of stability, order, harmony, self-sufficiency, and self-governance. This is the representation of it that we find in the writings of Mahatma Gandhi and Jayaprakash Narayan. But it did not go unchallenged. It was clinically and mercilessly demolished in a celebrated speech made by Dr B.R. Ambedkar in the Constituent Assembly. 'I hold that these village republics have been the ruination of India. I am therefore surprised that those who condemn provincialism and communalism should come forward as champions of the village. What is the village but a sink of localism, a den of ignorance, narrow-mindedness and communalism?' (Constituent Assembly Debates 1989: vol. 7, p. 39).

My own fieldwork in a south Indian village where I lived in 1961–2 (Béteille 1965) convinced me that Dr Ambedkar's view of it was far closer to the reality than the view of it as a harmonious and unchanging little republic. Other community studies made by my colleagues and students in the 1960s and 1970s confirmed my belief that Dr Ambedkar's view was substantially correct (Chakravarti 1975; Bliss and Stern 1982; Madan 2002). It is now nearly 60 years since Dr Ambedkar made his statement in the Constituent Assembly, and the Indian village has undergone many changes during this period, but it is doubtful that the divisions and inequalities of gender, caste, and class have disappeared without leaving any trace.

It is far from my intention to suggest that we should turn our backs on the Indian village and proceed through some other avenue if we are to promote elementary education in the country. We cannot do it, and we should not try to do it. All I am saying is that if we are to succeed in our endeavours, we must keep a close eye on the reality of the school and the community, and not allow social analysis to be displaced by ideology.

* * *

If the observations I have made appear somewhat vague and inconclusive, the fault does not lie entirely with me. In preparing this chapter, I have been handicapped by the lack of sustained critical discussion of the subject based on reliable empirical material. If such material exists, all I can say is that it is not easily available. I am aware that there is a growing body of statistical material on elementary education. That material answers a number of important questions, but it does not answer the questions that I have raised, which I believe are also important.

We have hardly any sustained research on the school as a social institution, as a field of social interaction with its internal strains and tensions; or of the school's relationship with the community and the wider society within which it exists. The relationship between school and society is replete with ambiguities. It is a complex and difficult subject of which social science research in India has barely scratched the surface. We do not have any satisfactory typology of schools beyond classifications made in purely formal terms such as size, material resources, and source and type of funding. It is difficult to see how we can have informed public discussion of elementary education in the absence of such research.

It is not easy to explain why research in the sociology of education and, particularly, on the social situation of the school has not received the serious attention it deserves. When sociological research began to expand in India 50 years ago, the small number of scholars who were entering the field devoted their attention to other areas of enquiry, and there were many of those to attract their attention. The modern school, including the elementary school, is an open and secular institution and, as such, is very different in its social texture from the traditional institutions based on kinship, caste, and religion. The success of open and secular institutions in India will depend in no small measure on how well the school socializes its pupils for participation in forms of interaction that are very different from those to which their forefathers had been accustomed.

In the meantime, the orientation of research in sociology and related social science disciplines has changed from 'delayed-return' to 'immediate-return' research (Béteille 2006). The kind of research on the sociology of the school that I have in mind that will explore the nature of interactions within the school is 'delayed-return research', and it is no longer popular today.

Social scientists in the universities often complain that there is no money for social science research. This is not entirely true. There is more money for research now than there was 50 years ago, but most of it is for 'immediate-return' research. Funding agencies have become result oriented; they not only want results, they want quick, not to say immediate, results. The forms of research are maintained in terms of sample size, design of questionnaire, and so on, but the results are often trivial and lead to little new insight. This kind of research is being increasingly organized by agencies outside the universities which do not generally have a long-term commitment to the accumulation of intellectual capital. They see their main obligation as the submission of project reports to the funding agencies.

'Delayed-return' research is costly, not so much in terms of money as of effort and time. It aims at the accumulation of knowledge on a long-term basis; its course is uneven and its outcome not always guaranteed. It cannot clearly anticipate its outcome in advance and say whether that outcome will be of immediate practical benefit or mainly of intellectual value, or neither.

I do wish to emphasize that serious research is costly in the sense that it does not always lead to a fruitful outcome. Where it comes to a subject of such immediate practical concern as elementary education, the funding tends to flow to agencies outside the universities, and the universities are generally out of funds. Yet, a deeper and more comprehensive understanding of education cannot come without a long-term investment in research, and without that understanding, public action will lack direction. The fact that research does not always lead to fruitful or practical outcomes cannot be an argument against supporting it on a long-term basis.

Advance is being made in the spread of elementary education and various parties are contributing to the advance. Greater advance requires wider participation. There is no doubt that the advance needs to be monitored through the collection and analysis of data on a more extensive basis. This kind of monitoring is necessary to enable people to know how well particular policies or programmes are working. Funding agencies, whether within or outside the government, would naturally like to know whether the resources being put into education are producing the expected results. What I am asking for is something more than this, which is research that can tell us whether and to what extent long-term shifts are taking place in the relationship between the institutions of education and the communities in which they are embedded.

Long-term advances cannot take place without changes in the structure of communities and without the creation of durable institutions for learning and teaching. There are no recipes available either for changing the structure of communities or for creating durable institutions. But little progress will be made unless we get to know better how communities are organized today and how institutions actually operate within them.

References

Béteille, André. 1965. *Caste, Class and Power*. Berkeley: University of California Press.

———. 2006. 'Sociology and Current Affairs', *Sociological Bulletin*, vol. 55, no. 2, pp. 201–14.

Bliss, C. and N. Stern. 1982. *Palanpur*. New Delhi: Oxford University Press.

Boudon, Raymond. 1974. *Education, Opportunity and Social Inequality*. New York: John Wiley.

Bourdieu, Pierre and Jean-Claude Passeron. 1977. *Reproduction in Education, Society and Culture*. Beverley Hills: Sage Publications.

Chakravarti, Anand. 1975. *Contradiction and Change*. New Delhi: Oxford University Press.

Constituent Assembly Debates. 1989. *Official Report*, vol. 7. New Delhi: Lok Sabha Secretariat.

Devine, Fiona. 2004. *Class Practices*. Cambridge: Cambridge University Press.

Erikson, R. and J.H. Goldthorpe. 1993. *The Constant Flux*. Oxford: Clarendon Press.

Jencks, Christopher et al. 1979. *Who Gets Ahead?* New York: Basic Books.

Madan, Vandana (ed.). 2002. *The Village in India*. New Delhi: Oxford University Press.

Chapter 6

Access to Education*

There have been large and significant changes in the scope and organization of education throughout the world in the last 200 years. There are now more schools, colleges, universities, and other institutions of learning than ever before, and more persons attend such institutions at present than at any time in the past. These changes first began in Western countries such as Britain, France, and the United States where they accompanied changes in the economic and political orders. It is now a truism that both democracy and development require a comprehensive and inclusive system of education.

Although the expansion of education began in those countries that first experienced the industrial and democratic revolutions, it is now taking place practically everywhere. There is hardly any country in the modern world that would not like to have a comprehensive and inclusive system of education. Yet, the expansion of education

*This is the text of the Kamala Lecture delivered at the University of Calcutta on 18 February 2008. I am grateful to the authorities of the university for inviting me to deliver this very important lecture named after the daughter of the redoubtable Sir Ashutosh Mukherji. It was subsequently published in *Economic and Political Weekly*, vol. XLIII, no. 20, 17 May 2008, pp. 148–56.

Earlier versions of the lecture were presented at the National University of Educational Planning and Administration, IIT Madras, IIT Guwahati, and the University of Bombay. I have benefited much from the discussions generated by the lecture at these places.

has not followed the same course everywhere, and in some countries it has been highly uneven. Access to education is not easy under all circumstances and, where it is made easy, the quality of the education provided often leaves much to be desired.

The drive for the expansion of education comes from various sources. Idealists believe that the advancement of learning, which is the motto of the University of Calcutta, should be an end in itself. Planners and policymakers have more practical considerations in mind. Every modern or modernizing society presents challenges and problems to its citizens that cannot be addressed without a minimum of schooling: filling forms, writing applications, reading notices, and so on. Such basic skills can of course be imparted and acquired in the family or the community. But most societies today find it more convenient to organize teaching and learning, even at the elementary level, through institutions entrusted with specifically educational functions. The growth of specifically educational institutions has been both a cause and a consequence of changes in the family and the community.

In the early stages of economic and political advance, the gap between the lettered and the unlettered is large and conspicuous. It is no less significant than the gap between the propertied and the propertyless. Many people manage reasonably well without owning any land or capital, but life is severely circumscribed for those who are unlettered and unschooled. In the advanced industrial countries, where first elementary and then secondary education became universal, the economic, political, and social significance of the disparity between the schooled and the unschooled has become greatly reduced. But this has not happened everywhere, and the proportion of children who have never been to school stands out today as an important indicator of a country's backwardness.

Indian society had a deeply hierarchical structure in which life chances were more unequally distributed than perhaps in any other society in the world. Even after the adoption of a modern system of education with its schools, colleges, and universities in the middle of the nineteenth century, access to education remained highly restricted for a hundred years, not only on account of severe economic inequalities but also because of strong and deeply rooted social prejudices against women and against disadvantaged castes and communities. Colonial rule served to ease some of the social prejudices but did little to address existing inequalities in the distribution of material resources.

The hierarchical structure of Indian society was such that inequalities between individuals and households were overshadowed by disparities between castes and communities. These disparities have not disappeared. Rather, democratic politics has brought them increasingly into public view in the last 60 years. Where access to education is concerned, the political leadership has given more attention in recent years to the redress of social disparities between communities than to the reduction of economic inequalities between individuals.

The Indian leadership viewed the coming of independence as an opportunity for a new beginning in the field of education. Many of the leaders were critical of the colonial system for what it did—or failed to do—in the cause of education in the country. Some, like Gandhi, wanted the system then in operation to be replaced by one that would be more in tune with the Indian tradition and serve the needs of the common people instead of creating and fostering a socially competitive middle class. Others, like Nehru and Ambedkar, were modernists and wanted the educational system not only to serve the common people but also to produce scientists and scholars who could take their place among the best in the world.

* * *

Schools, colleges, and universities were already in existence at the time of independence, but they were very few and outside the reach of the vast majority of people. Well over half of the population was illiterate, and even elementary schools were too few to serve the needs of the population, not only in the villages but even in the towns and cities. The leaders of the nationalist movement were inclined to attribute this unsatisfactory state of affairs to colonial rule. While this may be partly true, the plain fact is that opportunities for schooling had been always restricted by the country's rigidly hierarchical social structure and, in particular, by the hierarchical attitudes to the pursuit of learning prevalent in it since time immemorial.

With independence, India adopted a republican Constitution which was clearly designed to repudiate the principle of hierarchy and put 'equality of status and of opportunity' in its place. The new Constitution had a part on Fundamental Rights and a part on Directive Principles of State Policy, and both had strong provisions for equality in them. Article 45 sought to provide for 'free and compulsory education for all children until they complete the age of fourteen years'. It has more recently been decided to make elementary education not just a matter of policy but also a matter of right.

The commitment to provide elementary education to all, made at the time of independence, has not been met until now. Other countries have moved ahead, but India has stayed behind. What India has achieved in the field of elementary education appears in a very poor light when compared with the industrialized countries at comparable stages of economic development. The Indian experience shows that the failure to make elementary education universally available is a matter not only of material resources but also of social attitudes and orientations. Beneath the surface of public pronouncements, those attitudes and orientations continue to be deeply hierarchical, not least among those responsible for the operation of the educational system.

It is not that nothing has been achieved in the last 60 years. Literacy rates have gone up and, even though the rise has been slow, there is a secular trend of increase in literacy. Many new schools have come up, and there are many more children, both boys and girls, from an increasing range of castes and communities in school today. Official statistics mainly show the number of schools and the number of children enrolled in them. What they do not bring out are the disparities in the quality of education provided by schools of different kinds. These disparities are very large and probably increasing.

Those concerned at the time of independence with the advance of education did not confine their attention to only elementary and secondary education. They were, if anything, even more concerned with the creation and expansion of the institutions of higher education. India had made a reasonably good start with universities nearly a hundred years before independence, but the Indian universities were too few in number to satisfy the needs of an aspiring and assertive middle class, not to speak of the population as a whole.

* * *

The new government signalled its interest by setting up, almost immediately after independence, a University Education Commission under Dr S. Radhakrishnan, who was to soon become the first vice-president of the republic and thereafter its second president. New universities and centres of excellence in study and research were planned and put in place. Among these were the Indian Institutes of Technology (IITs) and the Indian Institutes of Management (IIMs) which now attract some of the best talent in the country. The number of universities has increased many times in the last 60 years, and to these we have to add the deemed universities such as the Tata Institute of Social Sciences as well as the Institutes of National Importance such as the Indian Statistical Institute.

It has often been pointed out that the universities in the pre-independence period were creatures of the colonial government. They were established by the government, funded directly by the government, and regulated by it. Hence, even where they attracted scientists and scholars of great ability and talent, their autonomy as institutions was limited. Today, Sir Ashutosh is still remembered for the way in which he protected and promoted the principle of autonomy in the University of Calcutta.

The University Grants Commission (UGC) was set up in 1956 to provide some cushion to the universities in their negotiation with the government for funding. The UGC was set up under an Act of Parliament, and it was expected to function in such a manner as to protect the autonomy of the individual universities under its care. It was also expected to uphold and promote excellence in teaching and research by overseeing the work of the universities through independent committees. Its success in these matters has been limited, and many now complain that it has become increasingly intrusive over the years.

Even while the universities were receiving public support, some began to feel that things were not going well with elementary and secondary education. Particularly in a large and populous country like India, the universities cannot stand on their own. They depend for their intake on what is produced by the schools. When the schools do not do their work adequately, teaching at an advanced level, not to speak of research, becomes hard to sustain. By the time students enter the universities, they are already young adults and disciplined habits of academic work are difficult to create at that age. Remedial education is useful for certain limited and specific purposes, but it cannot create afresh the general base for higher education if the schools have failed to create it through neglect or lack of direction.

A second commission, the Education Commission, was set up in 1964 under Dr D.S. Kothari. The Kothari Commission had the advantage of working with Indian as well as foreign experts of the highest standing. It produced a comprehensive report on all aspects of education. It dwelt on the linkages between the different levels of education, and on the connection between education and employment.

It is important to keep in mind the differentiation of the levels of education—primary, secondary, and tertiary—in the context of pressures to make access to education more open and easy. In advocating a more inclusive educational system, many argue as if the problems of access are more or less the same at all levels of the system. This is a mistake. The conditions of access change as we move up from one level of education to the next. I will illustrate this by considering the two extremes of the system, primary education at one end and postgraduate education at the other. What I will say here will apply, with appropriate qualifications, to all the levels in between.

In a democratic and secular society, access to primary education should be provided without consideration of race, caste, creed, and gender. Whether it should be made compulsory is a separate question into which I do not wish to enter here. No child, whether boy or girl, should be denied admission to a primary school. To what extent we should have mixed schools or allow separate schools for boys and girls or for children of different religious faiths is again a separate question.

Access to primary school should be granted to children also without consideration of merit, ability, or performance. Here I would like to point out that the two kinds of consideration for access to educational institutions, the first based on social and the second on scholastic grounds, are quite different. What I am trying to argue is that in the conditions under which we live today, restriction on neither kind of ground, social or scholastic, is justified at the point of entry into the educational system taken as a whole.

Some Indian schools, particularly in the major metropolitan cities, do indeed conduct tests of aptitude in order to sort out those they wish to admit from those they do not. This is an unhealthy practice and has become a bone of contention among many. No matter how much we deplore the practice, we have to examine the reasons for its prevalence. The number of applications in some schools is vastly in excess of the number of places available, whereas in other schools it is the opposite. Hence, schools that have a high reputation are constrained to deny admission to many, while at the other end, there are schools that have more places than they are able to fill. The way to reduce, if not eliminate, the unhealthy practice of testing for aptitude at the first point of entry is to set up more schools that provide primary education that will be to the satisfaction of most if not all parents. Society has an obligation to provide elementary education to all children, but whether it has the obligation to provide access in each case to an institution of the child's—or the parent's—choice is a different matter.

When we turn to the other end of the spectrum, that is, higher education, the problem changes its colour. To be sure, access to universities and other centres of advanced study should not be denied on grounds of race, caste, creed, or gender. But is it reasonable to expect such institutions to make admissions without consideration of ability and performance? The urge to make public institutions inclusive is understandable in a society that has practised exclusion so pervasively and so stringently over such a long span of time. But that urge cannot be allowed to subvert the very activities that particular institutions have been designed to perform.

To urge academic institutions to become more inclusive and at the same time to acknowledge that they need to impose restrictions on admissions (and appointments) appears self-contradictory to many who have little familiarity with the working of such institutions at different levels. But the contradiction is only apparent, and it dissolves when we recognize that educational institutions at different levels—the elementary school, the secondary school, the undergraduate college, the postgraduate department, and the centre of advanced study and research—though interlinked with each other, have different tasks to perform.

* * *

The contradictions a country with an expanding educational system faces are clearly revealed in the Report of the University Education Commission. These contradictions are particularly acute in India where a democratic political order based on the principle of equality was adopted in a country with a deeply hierarchical social order. In such a setting, divergent views are expressed by different persons, and sometimes by the same person in different contexts.

Dr Radhakrishnan's Commission said, 'Education is a universal right, not a class privilege' (University Education Commission 1950: 50).

But then it went on to say, 'Intellectual work is not for all, it is only for the intellectually competent' (ibid.: 98).

When the country became independent after a long period of colonial rule, its leaders looked forward to making education more widely, if not universally, available. The colonial administration had made a good beginning by creating new types of educational institutions—schools, colleges, and universities—but what it did was on a limited scale, and could hardly reach out to the entire population. I am aware that there are strong critics of the system of education designed for Indians by the British. Many things went wrong with the institutions they established, just as many things have gone wrong with the institutions created and managed by us in the last 60 years. But we owe something—not everything, but something—to the colonial regime for the creation of such institutions as Presidency College, Calcutta University, the Calcutta Medical College, the Law College in Calcutta, and the Bengal Engineering College. Even if they were created with the intention of serving the interests of colonial rule, their creation had momentous consequences for the regeneration of Indian society.

While we should not belittle the work done by the new schools, colleges, and universities in the hundred years preceding independence, we must recognize the relatively modest scope of their achievements. The policy objectives of the colonial administration were different from those of the government of independent India. Education was viewed by the former as being at best a beneficent instrument of social reform rather than a means for the radical transformation of a hierarchical society into one based on the principle of equality.

Rightly or wrongly, the British in India took the view that Indian society was hierarchical at its core with ineradicable inequalities among castes and communities and between men and women. Few of them really believed that changes in the educational system or in any other system could bring into being a completely different kind of society from the one that had been in existence since time immemorial. Their aim was not the spread of education among the masses but the creation of a small and accommodating middle class that would provide some scope for individual mobility to the fortunate few. In any case, it is doubtful that a colonial government would undertake the task of creating a 'casteless and classless society' anywhere in the world.

But the colonial government did sow the seeds of change in the Indian educational system. If we are concerned over the fact that women, Dalits, and members of the backward castes and communities are inadequately represented in our educational institutions today, honesty obliges us to admit that they were hardly present even in elementary schools a hundred years ago. A change had to take place in peoples' attitudes towards schooling, and that change began with the introduction of a modern educational system in the nineteenth century. The new system did not in fact provide equal opportunities for school admission to all, but its educational ideals were different from those of the past which were hierarchical and socially exclusive.

While the colonial administration set up schools, colleges, and universities, it invested only limited resources for their establishment and maintenance. In a highly stratified society this meant that opportunities for education, including secondary and even elementary education, were limited largely to the upper strata. Until the time of independence, education beyond the elementary level was virtually a monopoly of the middle class, and that class comprised a very small section of the population.

Although the new educational institutions were created at the initiative of the colonial administration, by the time the country became independent, their operation and management were in the hands of Indians. They had become the preserves of the upper strata of society in the provincial capitals and the district headquarters. There was some opening for individual mobility, but it was not very large. Because the medium of instruction at the higher levels was English, the division between the educated and the uneducated members of society became particularly marked.

The class composition of the educated sections changed, though not very radically, in the course of the hundred years prior to independence. When independence came, the high schools, the colleges, and the universities were in the control of the educated, professional middle class. But that was not exactly so in the beginning when that class was still to acquire a distinct social identity. The funding for the new educational institutions did not all come from the government. Wealthy Indians, particularly landowners and businessmen, made substantial contributions, and their offspring were prominent among the early beneficiaries of the new educational system.

The products of the new educational system found employment as school teachers, clerks, managers, officers, lawyers, and doctors, and formed the core of the new middle class whose offspring in turn enlarged the ranks of school, college, and university students. The sons of impoverished landowners sought employment in middle-class occupations, and for them the credentials provided by the new educational system became a necessity. The pressure for the expansion of the educational system and the credentials it provided came mainly from the middle class or aspirants for entry into it, and, as I have said, in the early years of the twentieth century they were still relatively small in number.

No middle class grows in size, no matter how limited the growth, without becoming internally differentiated and stratified. While a good secondary education was enough to secure a foothold in that class, it was not enough for entry into its higher ranks. For that, higher education, including professional education, was indispensable. Hence, pressure on the colleges and universities began to mount even before independence appeared in sight. Education and employment came to be closely linked. While a few may have sought university education for the pleasure of it, most wanted it because it was necessary for remunerative and respectable employment. All these considerations were still somewhat remote for the vast majority of Indians who lived from hand to mouth by some kind of manual employment for which formal education was not a requirement.

As I have noted, independence was accompanied by a surge of enthusiasm for spreading the benefits of education at every level to all classes and communities instead of letting them remain confined to the middle class. There was a contradiction in this, for the hold of the middle class over public institutions became stronger and not weaker in the wake of independence. The leaders of all political parties came from this class and there was no alien government to hold its ambitions in check. No middle class anywhere has attended to the interests of the other social classes before attending to its own. The middle class entered a path of all-round expansion, first through the growth of the public sector and then through that of the private sector. Aspirants for entry into it were hungry for higher education and even secondary education, and for them the availability of primary education was taken for granted. The requirements of primary education were never denied, they were largely ignored.

After a phase of somewhat sluggish growth in the early decades of independence, elementary education has been growing at a faster rate in the last 10 or 15 years. It has begun to receive wider attention and support. Apart from the government, this support now comes from the corporate houses as well as the voluntary sector. There is also greater international interest in the development of elementary education in the country.

The enlargement of the provisions for education has been accompanied by the differentiation of educational institutions. This differentiation is a continuous and unremitting process and must receive serious consideration. I am not speaking now of the differentiation between the different levels of the educational system, such as primary, secondary, and higher education, but about the differentiation of quality and standard at each level of the system. What feeds into every higher level of the educational system by way of student intake is a highly differentiated product, flowing out of a great variety of institutions at the level immediately below it.

Differentiation in teaching and learning begins at the level of elementary education. There is an enormous variety of institutions providing or meant to provide elementary education, but we have very little systematic knowledge of the ways in which they work or do not work. No doubt we have quantitative data about enrolment, dropout, years of schooling completed, and so on, but these tell us little about what happens in the school by way of interaction between teachers and pupils (See Chapter 5). Educated middle-class parents know a great deal about the kinds of schools to which they send their children or aspire to send them, but such schools are only the tip of the iceberg. Beneath that tip lies a vast submerged mass of institutions, driven by currents that often have little to do with education.

I would like to stress that middle-class parents have become acutely conscious about the need to give their children a head start in the matter of education. The search for a good school begins very early, well before the child is of age to enter elementary school. Here, those who live in the metropolitan cities have an advantage because that is where the most desirable schools are available. The most desirable schools, even for elementary education, are not only expensive but they are also exclusive, if for no other reason than that they are so much in demand. Such schools are materially well endowed and equipped, they have well-qualified teachers, and the regularity and routine of teaching and learning are more conscientiously observed in them than in many undergraduate colleges or postgraduate departments. Those who receive elementary education in such schools are generally well prepared for the next stage of education.

At the other end are primary schools in remote villages and city slums where hardly any teaching takes place, and what is learnt is quickly forgotten and of little value for the next level of education in secondary school. The material equipment available for elementary education varies enormously between schools of different types. But there are other and more important disparities than the purely material ones. School management is often lax, and the regularity and routine of school work is treated lightly and negligently.

More serious than the shortage of buildings, blackboards, and books is the negligence of teachers. On an average, on any working day, 25 per cent of teachers in elementary schools remain absent from work (Kremer et. al. 2006). This of course does not tell us what those who are present do while they are in the school. Apathy and indifference are widespread, and they are transmitted easily from teachers to pupils. Moreover, traditions of rote learning are very deeply rooted among both teachers and pupils, and rote learning can hardly be said to provide a sound basis for entry into a modern system of higher education.

The disparities which begin with primary school are carried forward to the level of secondary education and often magnified there. At the far end of the scale, in the metropolitan cities, there are very competitive institutions that provide education that is good enough to prepare their pupils for the best undergraduate education anywhere in the world. But these schools constitute a tiny minority, although they do provide some opportunities for upward mobility to talented pupils from the lower rungs of the middle class. As is well known, the ones most in demand among the middle classes are the English-medium schools, known for some odd reason as 'convent schools'. But even among such schools, there are wide variations in standards of teaching, including English teaching.

Not all schools in the country are English-medium schools. Some schools provide very good education in the regional language, but they are few in number and are losing out to the English-medium schools in the competition for the best pupils. The dynamic sections of the middle class that are driving forward India's economic growth want English-medium schools for their children. Elected political leaders and their intellectual camp followers may decry the fascination for

English-medium schools in public, but they will not oppose their growth seriously, seeking, instead, to find places in such schools for their own offspring.

In a secondary school, as the pupil progresses from one class to another, the prospect of examinations begins to loom large. For pupils and their parents, board examinations are a trial, and for teachers and the school management, they are a perennial source of vexation. They distract seriously from the ordinary course of teaching and learning. Testing and examining are indispensable components of all modern educational systems, but in India they tend to displace the main functions of education, which are learning and teaching. One important indication of this is the widespread suspicion and exposure of malpractices in examinations.

The pressure for successful performance in the board examinations is felt in every layer of the middle class, from the lowest to the highest, and the more the middle class expands, the more widely it will be felt. It is being felt increasingly in other social classes as well for board examinations are the gateway for entry into the middle class. Even self-employed persons, who do not need certification from the board, would like to have it if only for its social value. To be a member of the middle class without having passed the boards has become an anachronism, at least for the male members of society.

Of course, those who have achieved exceptional success in commerce or in the arts may occasionally boast that they have never passed a single examination.

Successful performance in the board examinations does not depend only on what is taught and learnt in school. In many secondary schools very little teaching is done, and students have to rely perforce on external assistance. Even those who go to the best schools try to secure external assistance, not so much to clear the board examinations as to be able to secure admission in the most coveted institutions at the next higher level. Once begun, the competition for places in the most coveted educational institutions acquires its own momentum. It is difficult to see how this competition can be avoided without abolishing the middle class, as happened, although briefly in China.

Various agencies outside the school are used for enhancing the pupil's competitive advantage. There is the coaching class, very familiar to me from my own school days in Calcutta (now Kolkata) nearly 60 years ago. These have multiplied and diversified enormously since those days and have spread to the small towns and even the larger villages. At least in Delhi, the best ones among them provide coaching not so much for success in the board examinations as for entry into the Indian Institutes of Technology (IITs) and other coveted institutions of higher study. Somewhat more expensive than the coaching class is private tuition for the individual pupil, either in his home or in the home of the tutor.

An important source of competitive advantage in tests and examinations is the family. Indian parents are very actively involved in the prospects of their children even after they have reached adulthood, and in the growing middle class these prospects have much to do with education and employment. Intellectual capital is very unevenly distributed among families, and two families with the same amount of it may devote very unequal attention to the educational advancement of their children.

Thus, different factors contribute to success or failure in the educational system, all the way up from primary to higher education. These factors include natural ability and aptitude; individual initiative and effort; the family's economic, social, and cultural capital; the pedagogic standards and practices of the school; and the care and attention the pupil receives from the school, the family, and the community. They may operate against each other or reinforce each other. The resulting inequalities in educational performance may be mitigated to some extent by well-designed policies, but they cannot be wished out of existence. Any policy that fails to take serious account of the disparities between different educational institutions and the inequalities in the wider society of which they are a part is bound to be infructuous.

* * *

If we turn to the other end of the scale and look at the university as an institution of higher study and research, we will appreciate why the conditions of access to it have to be different from those that are appropriate for the primary school. The conditions of access to higher education vary from one country to another and they have also changed over time. In some countries, such as the United States today, a very large proportion of the population is able to secure the benefits of higher education, although even there that was not the case until 50 or 60 years ago. In India, the benefits of higher education remain outside the reach of the vast majority of people. However, no matter how wide the access to universities may be, in no country do they give admission without requiring some evidence of prior academic qualification. Even in the United States, where access to higher education is wider than in any other country, no student can count on admission to the university of his choice unless he has the requisite test scores or the capacity to pay, or both.

In the modern world, education and employment are closely linked everywhere, even in the most affluent countries. The pressure on the universities, especially in countries like India, would not be so acute if a university degree did not come with the promise of employment in superior non-manual occupations. The fact that the promise is not always fulfilled is a different matter. No one can seriously expect to secure employment in a professional, managerial, or administrative occupation without a university degree. One may of course live on rental income or start an independent business, but even there a university degree is a useful thing to have.

People say that university degrees have become steadily devalued in the last 60 years, and this is probably true to some extent. In the early decades of the last century and even until the time of independence, university graduates enjoyed a certain social standing whether or not they were able to secure remunerative employment. The mounting pressure on the colleges and universities to admit more students and produce more graduates has led to a certain loss of credibility in many institutions of higher education. They have been forced under pressure to relax their standards of examination, and, what is worse, reduce teaching to the bare minimum required for clearing examinations.

University graduates no longer enjoy the social standing they did in the past, partly because their ranks have become greatly swollen. This has happened also because it has become increasingly manifest that it is now possible to secure a university degree without receiving much by way of a university education. The fact that a person no longer needs to be properly educated in order to be a graduate is by now fairly well known, yet the pressure on the universities to produce more BAs, more MAs, and now more PhDs continues unabated. A university degree by itself may be worth little economically, but no person is worth very much socially without one.

It is said that the university set up by Wilhelm von Humboldt in Berlin in 1810 was the first modern university. Humboldt's university was based on the principle of the unity of teaching and research. Until his time, the universities had concentrated mainly on teaching and undertook very little systematic research. The University of Berlin became a model for universities in Europe, America, and elsewhere. Today all universities are expected to combine teaching with research, although they do so in varying proportions and with varying degrees of success.

The Indian universities began differently. At the universities of Calcutta, Bombay, and Madras, all established in 1857, hardly any research was done in the nineteenth century. Not much teaching was done in them either. The teaching was conducted in the colleges, a few of which were set up before the universities. The main functions of the universities, when they started, were to design courses of study, set up boards of examiners, conduct examinations, and confer degrees. The first controllers of examinations were appointed before the first university professors. Even today the function of the controller of examinations remains crucial and his office is often like a fortress.

Teaching and research began to expand slowly, and some islands of excellence, as at the University of Calcutta in the second quarter of the last century, began to emerge. At least in the better universities, teaching and research held their ground for some time against the rush for more and more degrees at any price. The rush has gained momentum in the last couple of decades under political pressure.

The pressure for the expansion of higher education comes from various quarters. The government wants more graduates to meet the needs of a rapidly expanding economy, and the growing middle class wants more places in the colleges and universities for its offspring. The number of colleges and universities has multiplied many times in the last 60 years. Apart from there being many more universities, new kinds of universities, with somewhat more specialized functions than the older ones, are now coming up. The earlier universities were built around a core of disciplines in the arts and sciences to which other disciplines, such as law and medicine, were added. In addition to those, there are now agricultural universities, universities of science and technology, universities of health sciences, law universities, and universities of information technology.

When one expands from 30 to 300 universities within a span of 60 years, one cannot expect all universities to create and maintain the same standards in teaching and research. There are various reasons why those standards are highly uneven in our colleges and universities. There are vast disparities in material resources: buildings, libraries, laboratories, and so on. But there are also enormous disparities in the capabilities of the students they admit and the teachers they appoint.

The universities have to contend with contradictory pressures. There is, first, the pressure to build up excellence on a selective basis, and there is also the pressure to allocate resources on an equitable if not uniform basis. In recent decades, it is the second kind of pressure that has grown and mounted while the first has often been reduced to a residual status.

Some university institutions have very good facilities. IIT Madras has a splendid campus, a well-equipped library, and excellent laboratories. The Jawaharlal Nehru University also has good facilities. But this is far from the case with most universities, including some central universities whose libraries are stocked mainly with text books, and even those are of somewhat ancient vintage. Pressures for the admission of more students and the appointment of more teachers have generally outstripped the provisions for expanding material facilities on a proportionate scale. The money that comes in from the government is limited, and most of it goes into salaries and basic services such as water and electricity, with very little left for libraries and laboratories.

Even more important are the disparities in ability and aptitude among both teachers and students in colleges and universities in the different parts of the country. There is an enormous range of variation in ability among teachers and aptitude among students. The variations are not random, but structured in such a way that a few institutions attract both teachers and students of high quality while most have to make do with what is left over, which is of very indifferent quality. There are grounds to believe that the number and proportion of persons of poor or indifferent quality have increased steadily in recent decades both absolutely and as a proportion of the total. It is here that we have to remind ourselves of Dr Radhakrishnan's observation that intellectual work is not for all but for the intellectually competent, even though such an observation is not likely to find favour with any political party today.

Many institutions of higher education are marked by a general atmosphere of apathy and lassitude, which is relieved from time to time when there is a festival, an agitation, or a strike. Students often stay away from classes because they do not feel the need to attend them in order to pass their examinations. There are many absentee teachers in our universities who use academic appointments as sources of rental income. The fact that more and more persons want to enrol in colleges and universities does not mean that they are there to advance their knowledge of the arts and sciences; many of them come for the degrees which they hope will secure them gainful employment. Similarly, teachers do not seek places in colleges and universities because they all have a vocation for science or scholarship, but because they see them as sources of gainful employment or rental income, and because they have political promoters who want academic institutions to create more openings for members of their caste or community or their electoral constituents.

It is natural for students to be deterred from attending classes when they find that they are unable to follow what is being taught. Many students are unable to follow what is being taught simply because they have not had the kind of schooling that could prepare them to meet the demands of undergraduate education. There are helpful teachers in many colleges who are prepared to relax the standards of teaching even in honours courses in order to accommodate their ill-equipped students. But then, when those students seek to pursue postgraduate studies in a reputed institution, their lack of intellectual equipment comes to the surface again. What is an academic problem finds some kind of a political solution through pressures for the relaxation of standards overall.

The pressure from ill-prepared and ill-equipped students for admission into the institutions of higher education is relentless. It originates in the middle class and on its fringes, and is transmitted to the college and university authorities by those who control the machineries of government and politics. Over the years, university and college authorities have lost the will to resist these pressures and protect their academic standards. When they are faced with demands to expand their capacity, they bargain with the government for more funds in the spirit of managers who have to expand their industrial capacity.

The political leadership finds it convenient to satisfy middle-class aspirations by opening more colleges and universities instead of attending to the more urgent need of expanding and upgrading elementary and secondary education. Moreover, college and university students are politically organized in a way in which school students are not. Students' unions are a force to reckon with in the running of the university, and particularly its examination system. The university authorities are reluctant to apply strict academic standards for fear of a political backlash if that hurts the interests of the student community or any organized section of it. Vice-chancellors are very anxious to avoid any action that might invite charges of discrimination from unsuccessful students and their political patrons.

Standards of evaluation for postgraduate degrees have been progressively relaxed in many, if not most, universities. I know more than one university where scarcely any candidate is failed and it is almost a matter of routine to give every candidate, or virtually every candidate, high second-class marks. This is a far cry from the days when Bankimchandra had to be given grace marks to clear the MA examinations, being the only person to do so in his year.

The situation is not very different at the level of the PhD degree. Uniformity of standards is, in any case, very difficult to maintain here since PhD theses are examined case-by-case instead of in batches. Here the decline of standards has been less due to organized pressure than to negligence and indifference among supervisors and examiners. Yet, the hunger for PhD degrees remains unabated. Despite the devaluation of university degrees, even persons outside the academic profession, including civic and political dignitaries, are eager to attach the title of 'doctor' to their names, and there are coaching centres to assist them in their endeavours.

No university system can hold its own in the modern world if it confines itself only to the transmission of existing knowledge and contributes nothing to the creation of new knowledge. Doctoral programmes aim to initiate young scholars and scientists into the challenging and exacting processes that lead to the creation of new knowledge. We have added a large number of new universities in the last 60 years but whether there has been a proportionate increase in the creation of new knowledge in them remains a matter of doubt.

It can of course be said that the purpose of setting up new universities is not simply to contribute to the creation of new knowledge but also to make our public institutions socially more inclusive by providing increasing space in them for the accommodation of all the classes and communities that constitute the larger Indian society. It is undeniable that our universities are not nearly as socially inclusive as universities in any modern society are expected to be. In this they reflect the hierarchy in the wider society and in the institutions of elementary and secondary education to which I drew pointed attention in the earlier part of the chapter. The manner in which our schools have been allowed to develop has had the inevitable consequence of generating huge inequalities in the conditions of competition at the point of entry into higher education. To try to rectify those inequalities through crash programmes for making the universities socially more inclusive can end only in frustration.

Our present political leadership believes that the main social responsibility of the universities is to produce more and more graduates so that middle-class employment is more evenly distributed among all classes and communities. There is remarkable agreement on this across the entire political spectrum. No political party seriously believes that creating new knowledge is a major social responsibility of the university or even that our universities are capable of doing so. Having allowed the university's intellectual capital to run down, they now say that since they do not in any case produce good scholars or good scientists, they might as well make themselves socially more inclusive and more representative. They can give more attention to their intellectual tasks after that objective has been achieved.

Modern societies have been described as knowledge societies. Their advance is believed to depend more on the accumulation and deployment of intellectual than of material capital. The creation and transmission of new knowledge takes place continuously and at an escalating pace. The universities of the twenty-first century have to operate in an intellectual environment that is radically different from that of the nineteenth century and earlier (Shils 1992). Earlier universities acted more as repositories of traditional knowledge than as workshops for the creation of new knowledge. Advances in knowledge no doubt took place in the past, but the universities absorbed those advances at a leisurely pace. This they can hardly afford to do if they are not to fall behind and stay behind. No argument for inclusiveness should be allowed to override all considerations of ability and performance in the institutions of advanced study and research.

In earlier times the universities could afford to suspend or relax their effort to keep pace with the advance of knowledge in the interest of some other social objective and expect to pick up the threads after a generation or two. To do so today will be a costly and hazardous venture. We will see other countries where universities were set up after ours overtake us and leave us behind. The Indian universities face a difficult and uncertain future. They must expand and multiply, and they must be socially inclusive. But if they are to retain credibility as centres of science and scholarship, they must also be selective in appointments and admissions and in the award of degrees. As centres of learning in an open society, they have an obligation to explain to the public why and in what sense being selective in academic matters is in principle different from practising discrimination on grounds of gender, community, and class. No modern university can tolerate discrimination on social grounds; nor can it survive as a centre of science and scholarship if it fails to discriminate, 'without fear or favour', on academic grounds.

References

Kremer, Michael et al. 2006. *Teacher Absence in India*. Harvard University (Working Draft).

Shils, Edward. 1992. 'The Service of Society and the Advancement of Learning in the Twenty-First Century', *Minerva*, vol. XXX, no. 2, pp. 242–68.

University Education Commission. 1950. *Report*, vol. 1. New Delhi: Government of India (Ministry of Education).

Chapter
7

The Making of an Inclusive Society*

Can we expect India to reach the goal of an inclusive society? This question is now increasingly asked by those who take a sympathetic interest in the country and its future. I will attempt to address the question here, even though I am unable to offer any exact definition of an inclusive society but only a rough sense of what we might mean by it. All societies are at best more or less inclusive, some more than others, ours being one of the least inclusive among societies in the contemporary world.

Indian society continues to be marked by extremes of inequality in the distribution of life chances. Large sections of the population in both rural and urban areas lack the resources and the capabilities to lead a meaningful social existence. Absolute poverty may have declined somewhat, but relative poverty still remains very large. Access to higher education and superior professional, managerial, and administrative occupations is still highly restricted. It is this limitation of access that people have in mind when they point to India's failure to become an inclusive society. But I am going to ask whether this is the only, or even the principal, matter to be considered when we seek a path towards being a more inclusive society.

It is not that the country has made no advances in the last 60 years. It is particularly in the light of those advances that its failure

*This is the text of a lecture organized jointly by the New India Foundation and *The Telegraph* in Kolkata on 6 March 2009.

to achieve significant changes in the distribution of life chances appears glaring and insupportable.

A quick review of the advances made so far may be useful at this point. The economy has maintained a high rate of growth in the last couple of decades and, even if some setbacks occur, there is the confidence that comes from the widespread recognition that India is on the way to becoming an economic powerhouse. The condescension with which the country was viewed by the providers of development aid has become muted.

The recognition of India's economic capacity has been accompanied by the acknowledgement of its right to develop its nuclear technology for multiple uses. India has made its way into the charmed circle of the countries that can use nuclear technology for civilian purposes and, in principle, also for military purposes.

These would be important achievements in themselves, but what gives them special significance is that they have been accomplished within the framework of a democratic legal and political order. There were many who were sceptical about the prospects for democracy in India when the country became independent. But the course of events in the last 60 years has largely confounded the sceptics. There have been many ups and downs in the political system, leading to a great deal of confusion and alarm, but democracy has survived, not just in form but also in substance.

The Indian tradition has been tolerant of diversity and dissent, and the success of democracy in India has been attributed by many to the vitality of that tradition. A democratic system is by its nature subject to conflicting pulls and pressures. It has to respond to a variety of interests which demand attention simultaneously. Hence, while progress and advance do take place, the course of change tends to be slow and uneven. India is often compared to its great neighbour China, and in terms of economic growth and military capability, the comparison is to China's advantage. But China's economic and military advantage is in no small measure due to its unitary and conformist political system which leaves little room for dissent in public life. For how long this kind of political system can survive in the face of an economy which is driven by relentless competition among individuals and groups, only the future can tell.

It is not enough to have a tradition of dissent. For democracy to function as a political system, dissent must be given an institutional form. The institutions specifically associated with the operation of democracy in India are not all of ancient provenance but have nevertheless become a part of the political process. Many of the new ones are yet to acquire secure foundations in the country. The challenge is to create an inclusive society without compromising the new political institutions that are essential for making democracy stable and lasting.

Government and opposition are both considered legitimate and necessary components of the political system in India today. Such a system must necessarily make room for a diversity of parties, associations, platforms, policies, and doctrines. A one-party system or a system which allows the expression of only a single point of view or demands exclusive loyalty to a single leader is antithetical to the spirit of democracy.

A democratic system is an open system to the extent that it allows rival political formations to contend openly with each other. There are two aspects of India's character as an open society that I would like to stress. The first, which I have already indicated, is the tolerance and even the encouragement of diversity in political organization, and the second is the wide and active participation of the people in the competition for political power and authority.

Democracy has enabled Indians not only to uphold and promote every viewpoint and agenda, but also to participate more or less freely in a wide range of political activities. The changes in attitudes and perceptions brought about through the participation of hitherto marginalized or stigmatized sections of the population cannot be denied or ignored. Processions, rallies, and demonstrations in support of one or another political cause, and generally against those in authority, have become a conspicuous feature of public life in India.

Our general elections have received wide attention and coverage nationally and internationally. Their significance in the life of the nation cannot be too strongly emphasized. The electoral process is open and transparent, though not always very orderly. Despite persistent allegations of malpractice and occasional bursts of violence, they are reasonably free and fair. Voter turnout has been uneven, but it has generally been on the high side. Voters have braved inclement weather and even threats of violence in order to exercise their franchise. High voter turnout has been noted in all parts of the country, and in both rural and urban areas.

Many have commented on the festive atmosphere that prevails on election day, particularly in the rural areas and among the poorer folk.

It provides people with a kind of relief from the monotony and drudgery of everyday life. But voters in India do exercise their choice. They can be wilful, intractable, and unpredictable as candidates who have taken their support for granted have learnt to their cost again and again.

It will be shallow and misleading to dismiss the festive atmosphere of election day as a kind of ritual of reversal. The ordinary voter, whether peasant, worker, or housewife, does periodically contribute to the downfall of an incumbent legislator or minister. But that does not change everything. Indeed people have pointed out repeatedly that our periodic elections have done little to bring about any real change in the social order or to shake it out of its hierarchical mould. They have led to the replacement of one set of leaders, or one political party in office, by another, but have left largely unaltered the inequalities in the distribution of life chances and even the distribution of power between the different classes and strata that make up our society.

* * *

Thus, while India appears as an open society when we look at the political system, the barriers to access are so extensive and so pervasive that it can hardly be described as an inclusive society in any meaningful sense. The mismatch between the democratic political system created at the time of independence and the hierarchical social order inherited from the past has been the main obstacle to the creation of an inclusive society in India.

I have already referred to the tolerance of diversity in the past as an enabling condition for the success of democracy in the present. Diversity prevailed not only in customs and practices but also in ideas, beliefs, and values. But the diversity that was allowed to prevail was organized hierarchically and not democratically. Social gradations were widespread and elaborate, and they were maintained by a multitude of exclusionary practices. This very significant aspect of the traditional order tends to be ignored or overlooked by those who maintain that it was congenial to democracy. Support for exclusionary practices ran through India's pluralist social and cultural order, from the top to the bottom.

The caste system epitomized social exclusion in its most extreme and elaborate form. Here I shall use the term in the broad sense to include, in addition to castes in the strict sense, tribes, sects, and other groups based on a strong sense of collective identity and occupying more or less distinct positions in the wider social order; indeed, the term caste has been extended to other societies wherever social exclusion was practised in a conspicuous form (Dollard 1957). But neither the system of Apartheid in South Africa nor the system of racial stratification in the US South had the elaborate formal structure of the Indian caste system, and neither endured nearly as long. Moreover, the social exclusion of women was carried much further in India than elsewhere; but this is a subject into which I cannot enter any further here.

In the past, social exclusion was clearly marked by the physical disposition of communities. The Adivasis or Scheduled Tribes were isolated in remote and inaccessible areas whereas the Harijans or Scheduled Castes were segregated in their own quarters in the village or town. Despite the many changes that have taken place in India since independence, the marks of both isolation and segregation are in evidence in village, town, and city in virtually every part of the country.

Since ancient and medieval times, Indian society has been built through the slow but steady accommodation of diverse groups that were allowed to retain their distinctive identities even while they became parts of a larger whole. Accommodation without assimilation is what gave to Hindu society its distinctive character. According to N.K. Bose (1975), this process was not seriously disturbed during the long period of Muslim rule, as Muslim communities fitted themselves into the pattern that had become securely established in the land. It was the joint operation of the new economic system and the new legal order ushered in by British rule that began to undermine the traditional social arrangements.

Many of the communities that made up the larger Indian society existed on its peripheries both geographically and culturally. They maintained their own forms of speech, their own religious practices, and their own modes of livelihood. They constituted what came to be known as the tribal population of India. The distinction between tribe and caste has been difficult to formulate conceptually for the reason that the boundaries between the tribal communities and the wider society were always porous. Interchanges in the economic as well as the cultural spheres have taken place across these boundaries since time immemorial.

N.K. Bose sought to identify the characteristics of what he called 'the Hindu method of tribal absorption'. He showed how tribal communities entered into economic relations with their technologically more advanced neighbours and gradually adopted some of their social and cultural practices without ever giving up their distinctive collective identities. In course of time, according to him, a tribe came to be treated as a caste. This process, which was witnessed by ethnographers until the middle of the last century, had been in operation since the time of the Mahabharata. The social order of Hinduism was a hierarchical one, and when a tribe was transformed into a caste, it was generally assigned a lowly position in the hierarchy.

In Bose's representation, the Hindu method of tribal absorption was not only slow and gradual, but it was also a peaceful one. But it is unlikely that the tribal people always chose remote and inaccessible places for their habitation of their own free will. Sometimes they were pushed into those areas by their more aggressive and better organized neighbours. Moreover, their own areas of habitation were periodically penetrated and settled by non-tribal populations. But the point about the co-existence of tribal and non-tribal communities in India is that, despite many interchanges between them, each community maintained its distinctive collective identity.

The transformation of tribes into castes, which took place throughout Indian history, went into decline in the course of the twentieth century, and has now lost much of its motive force. The tribal communities, or at least their political leaders, no longer wish for accommodation in the hierarchical order of Hindu society at its lowest level. The political process is in fact leading to reinforcement rather than weakening of collective identities in the tribal population throughout the country.

While the tribal people were socially excluded through isolation, the Harijans or Dalits were excluded through segregation. Most villages had segregated communities of Dalits, and this was true of towns and cities as well. They had a peculiar position in the life of the village, town, or city. They were indispensable to its economic life for they performed certain necessary economic functions. They were indispensable also to its ritual life because the Hindu obsession with purity and pollution required the presence of specialist groups for the treatment and removal of defiling matter so as to ensure the purity of the rest of the community.

In India, social exclusion was maintained to an unusual degree through the elaboration of rules relating to purity and pollution. Indian society was by no means unique in the practice of social exclusion. What was distinctive, if not unique, to it was the elaborate ritual idiom through which social exclusion was maintained and reproduced across the generations. The rules of purity and pollution restricted access to temples, wells, and even roads. They also set strict limits to social interchange, including, most notably, matrimonial exchange and the exchange of food and water.

The isolation of the Adivasis and the segregation of the Dalits were only the most extreme manifestations of social exclusion prevalent at all levels of the system. The principle and practice of exclusion permeated the entire social order. Its most characteristic focus was the restriction on intermarriage and inter-dining. Such restrictions were not confined only to the upper castes but were common also among the lower ones in their mutual relations. It is well known, for instance, that some Dalit castes denied access to their wells to other castes of the same or nearly the same rank (Patel 1973).

Social exclusion was generally associated with social ranking but not necessarily so. Castes or even sub-castes of roughly the same rank were often careful in maintaining on a reciprocal basis restrictions not only on intermarriage but also on inter-dining. I noted many such restrictions in the relations between the Smartha and the Shri Vaishnave Brahmins in the course of my fieldwork in a Tanjore village in 1961–2. They were still carefully maintained by many of the Brahmins of the older generation, although the restrictions on inter-dining were being eased among younger persons.

When we look back on our past, what we see again and again is that social exclusion was not just a matter of practice but also a matter of principle. It was upheld by both law and custom. This was not unique to India. Social exclusion was upheld by law and custom in all hierarchical societies, including medieval Europe and medieval China. Those societies have now changed. Is it possible that Indian society may also change?

* * *

The hierarchical order of society began to give way to a new kind of social order from the end of the eighteenth century onwards. Major changes were set in motion by the French Revolution and the Industrial Revolution acting more or less at the same historical juncture. These changes had their beginnings in the Western world—England, France, and the United States—but their effects came to be felt all across the world in course of time. Although the currents of change have had an impact worldwide, they have not operated with the same intensity or for the same length of time in all parts of the world. Moreover, each country has responded to the challenges presented by the new economic and political currents according to its own history and its own social structure.

The general trend of change was from a closed hierarchical type of society to a more open and democratic type. New legal and political institutions sought consciously to extend equality as a right and as a policy, and new economic opportunities for individuals began to undermine the inherited privileges and disabilities of the past. Exclusion from public life on grounds of race, caste, and creed ceased to be regarded as necessary or desirable. The twentieth century also witnessed a considerable change in the representation of women in public life.

The new age that first emerged in the West as a result of the joint operation of political and economic changes has come to be described as the age of democracy. When we speak of an age as the age of democracy, we have in mind not only a set of legal and political arrangements, but a whole social order with its own institutions, its own values and norms, and its own standards of everyday conduct. For democracy to be effective, we need not only new laws but also new attitudes of mind and new habits of the heart. It has proved more difficult to create these new habits and attitudes than to enact new legal rules.

The new society that began to emerge in the West along with the emergence of democracy was an open society and an inclusive one, at least in its aims and intentions. Its success has centred around two specific developments: the development of citizenship on the one hand, and the development of open and secular institutions on the other. These two together provide the essential ingredients of what I understand by civil society.

Under colonial rule, Indians were subjects and not citizens. But was citizenship an established feature of Indian society before the advent of colonial rule? I think it is essential to remember that since time immemorial our society has been a society of castes and communities and one in which the individual as citizen had but a minor place.

The emancipation of the individual—and women even more than men—from caste and community is a necessary condition for the growth of democratic citizenship and the institutions of civil society.

Any attempt to create a more inclusive society that leads to a reinforcement of caste and community is bound to weaken the claims of citizenship and to undermine civil society.

The point that needs to be stressed here is that citizenship is not a universal category of social existence but a historical category that emerged under specific conditions and gradually extended its appeal in the course of the nineteenth and twentieth centuries. The growth of citizenship has been associated with the creation of rights for the individual without consideration of race, caste, or community. The sociologist T.H. Marshall (1977: 71–134) traced the progression of these rights in Britain as the movement from civil rights in the eighteenth century to political rights in the nineteenth and, finally, to social rights in the twentieth century. Citizenship has acted as an equalizing tendency against the continuing and, sometimes, growing inequalities of class. The growth of citizenship played a major part in creating a more inclusive society in the West. However, universal citizenship, without consideration of race, caste, or creed has nowhere done away with the inequalities of class but only served to moderate them.

In India, the advance of citizenship has faced unprecedented resistance from the continuing vitality of kinship, caste, and community. As I have pointed out, under colonial rule, Indians were subjects and not citizens. The value of citizenship for the new republic was recognized in the Constituent Assembly. There is a separate part on citizenship in the Constitution of India which, in fact, comes immediately after Part I defining the Union and its territory. But making formal provisions for the rights of citizenship is one thing and making room for those rights to grow in the face of the strong countervailing claims of caste and community is another.

A society of castes and communities can make room for a society of citizens only with the emergence of a range of new legal, economic, educational, scientific, and other open and secular institutions. Such institutions are open in the sense that membership in them is not restricted by considerations of birth, and they are secular in the sense that they are not governed by religious rules or religious authorities. The germs of such institutions may have been present in Western countries for a long time, but they began to establish their predominance in public life only from the end of the eighteenth century onwards. They played an indispensable part in the consolidation of democracy as a social and not merely a political system. These open and secular institutions became the training grounds for democratic citizenship.

Open and secular institutions such as schools, colleges, hospitals, banks, municipal corporations, and professional and other associations began to emerge in India in the middle of the nineteenth century. At first their reach did not extend very far, being confined largely to the presidency capitals and the district headquarters. Some pointed out that they did not grow out of the Indian soil but were transplanted onto it from a different social environment. At the same time, it is difficult to see how a democratic political order can be sustained in our country if open and secular institutions fail to take root in it.

When the country became independent more than 60 years ago, the prospects for a new social order that would be compatible with the republican Constitution then being designed seemed good. Most people recognized that the modernization of India required the expansion of the existing modern institutions and the creation of new ones. The performance of our open and secular institutions, particularly those under the care of the state, has been at best uneven. Disorder has grown in public life and public institutions have failed to become socially inclusive in the natural course of their growth. Where political pressure has been applied from outside to make them socially more inclusive, their internal order and efficiency has been seriously compromised. Nothing demonstrates this more clearly than the state of our institutions of higher learning today.

* * *

Many factors contributed to the growth and advance of open and secular institutions in the West. The state played an important part, but not necessarily a dominant one. All Western countries did not follow the same trajectory. The state played a more prominent role as a promoter of inclusive and secular institutions in France than in Britain, not to speak of the United States. Napoleon's formula of 'careers open to talent' contributed much to the process of social churning that began in France in the nineteenth century.

Throughout the nineteenth century a new occupational system came to be established in the West and, in course of time, in most parts of the world. This occupational system was based on a new technology and a new organization of work. The division of labour became increasingly complex and increasingly elaborate. The location of the workplace in the office and the factory, and away from the home and the community, had profound consequences for society as a whole. The new organization of work did not put an end to economic inequality but it created great opportunities for individual mobility, both geographical and social.

A new educational system emerged alongside the new occupational system and partly in order to serve its requirements, particularly at the upper levels. Formal education, often over an extended period of time, became a necessary condition for entry into superior professional, administrative, and managerial occupations. Throughout the nineteenth century, the distinction between manual and non-manual employment was in large part a distinction between the unlettered and the lettered, and, for the latter, calibrated according to the type and amount of education.

Did England or France in the nineteenth century have an inclusive society? We have only to turn to the novels of Dickens or Balzac to appreciate the gulf between the unlettered class of manual workers and the educated middle class. Schooling had begun to expand but the expansion did not go far enough for any but the most talented or the most fortunate among the children of manual workers to benefit much from the promise of 'careers open to talent'. And, as for women, there was hardly any room for them in either the institutions of higher education or the liberal professions.

Barriers between classes and communities—and between men and women—became lowered as access to education and employment expanded in the twentieth century. Throughout the nineteenth century and well into the twentieth, it was America that was regarded as the land of opportunity. But in some respects the United States has been overtaken by a number of countries in Europe. The expansion of elementary and secondary education of reasonably good quality has played a major part in this outcome. Even where society has not become inclusive to the full extent, the more egregious forms of social exclusion have lost their force and sting.

The expansion of education at all levels created new opportunities as well as new attitudes of mind. Economic growth generated new kinds of employment as well as new avenues of mobility, both inter-generational and intra-generational. Industrial employment gained at the expense of agricultural employment, and non-manual at the expense of manual employment. A new middle class emerged and, as it expanded, provided accommodation within it to individuals with talent and ability from all sections of society. This middle class depended on the new open and secular institutions and also contributed to their growth.

It will be difficult to exaggerate the part played by the expansion of the new middle class in the making of a more inclusive society in the West. A significant feature of the middle class is the continuous flow of individuals and households across it. In all modern societies, the middle class is the breeding ground as well as the beacon of social mobility. The larger the size of the middle class, the greater the extent of mobility in a society. It is not that no mobility took place at all in the hierarchical societies of the past, but such mobility as took place there was slow, gradual, and limited in scope. It was experienced by only a few, and did not form a part of the general expectation.

The natural process of mobility through which hierarchical societies became more inclusive in other parts of the world—western Europe, the United States, and even east Asia—failed to gather sufficient momentum in India. Although new schools, colleges, and universities were established after independence, they failed to give the kind of boost to individual mobility that they were expected to give. Elementary education suffered from serious neglect, and, partly as a result of this, higher education contributed less to individual mobility than to the reproduction of inequality.

The expansion of the middle class and the growth in the scope and rate of individual mobility do not put an end to inequalities in the distribution of life chances. In no society is the middle class undifferentiated or unstratified. But the opportunities available for mobility vary greatly among stratified societies. Mobility acquires significance only when individuals are allowed and encouraged to compete with each other in the fields of education and employment; and it is a truism that where there is equality before the competition, there will be inequality after it. However, whether in education or in employment, the conditions of competition need not be such that large sections of the population are effectively denied the prospect of taking part in it.

The norms of citizenship cannot eliminate all inequalities of wealth, income, and occupation, and they should not be expected to do so. Those norms are important, not because they can guarantee equality in every respect, but because they are expected to prevent people from being pushed beyond the limits of a secure and meaningful life in society. The contradiction and the challenge in India today is that, despite 60 years of democracy and some considerable material advance in the last couple of decades, so many people still have to eke out an existence outside of those limits.

* * *

It is not my intention to argue that India has made no progress towards becoming a more inclusive society in the last 60 years. But the progress has been slow and uneven. Moreover, the path adopted for reaching the goal of an inclusive society has been the path of identity politics. This kind of politics has given far greater salience to the disparities between castes and communities than to the inequalities between individuals, households, and classes. Class politics has taken a back seat in the face of the steady advance of caste politics and minority politics (Béteille 2007).

There are two paths that appear to lead to an inclusive society. The first proceeds by expanding the rights of citizenship. The second proceeds by promoting the claims of castes and communities to fuller representation in public institutions. It is perhaps a mistake to believe that we can promote the claims of castes and communities indefinitely without putting any restraints on the claims of individuals as citizens.

The Indian political system has responded far more actively to the claims for representation in public institutions by the leaders of the backward castes and the minorities than to the need for creating better material conditions and better opportunities for the masses of disadvantaged individuals in the rural backwaters and the urban slums and shanty towns. Today, the various castes and communities are better represented in government and politics, and in the civil service and the universities than they were 60 years ago, and some of the credit for that goes to identity politics. But poverty, malnutrition, chronic ill health, and functional illiteracy have not disappeared or even declined to the extent that was expected 60 years ago. The material disparities between those elected or appointed to high office and the majority of the Indian people remain stark and glaring. In any democracy, the leaders live better than the ordinary people. In India they live exceptionally well in comparison to the hapless people on whose support they depend and in whose name they secure office and enjoy its benefits. This is true of the Indian political elite irrespective of caste and community.

Identity politics as the principal avenue for achieving social justice began to strengthen its hold over the public consciousness in the aftermath of the Emergency of 1975–7. Democracy survived the Emergency, but there was a shift in its wake from the constitutional to the populist form of it (Béteille 2008). Identity politics moved forward on the crest of a populist wave. Political leaders of all ideological persuasions came to recognize that it is easier to mobilize support on the basis of caste and community than on the basis of class. Identity politics has, in the last couple of decades, presented itself successfully as the true champion of social justice by pushing forward the demand for parity between castes and communities at the expense of the claims of the disadvantaged classes.

The seeds of identity politics were sown in India during the period of colonial rule. The British acted according to their own perceptions and their own interests. Their perception of Indian society was that it was in essence a society of castes and communities. They did not have any compelling desire, as the makers of our own Constitution did, of transforming India into a society of citizens. Nor was it only a question of perception. It suited their interest well to acknowledge and even strengthen the distinctions of caste and community so that they could maintain their own authority through a policy of 'divide and rule'.

The British introduced quotas in education and employment on the basis of caste and community well before the thought of India becoming a sovereign democratic republic had acquired a concrete form. Quotas were introduced for the Muslims mainly in north India and for the non-Brahmins mainly in the south. The British acted without any comprehensive plan for creating an inclusive society in India, and many of them were sceptical about the prospects for democracy in the country. Quotas were devised as a measure of prudence for governing an alien and unfamiliar population without too much trouble and too many risks.

Under colonial rule, quotas did not find favour with the leaders of the Congress, which spearheaded the nationalist movement (Bose n.d.). Those leaders made light of what quotas might contribute to equity and justice, and stressed their divisive role in public life. The British were aware of the nationalist argument, but did not yield to it.

They felt that it was only with quotas that they would be able to balance the claims and pressures that came from the leaders of the principal castes and communities.

Quotas were viewed with mistrust and suspicion for some time after the adoption of the new Constitution. After remaining subdued for some time, the demand for them picked up again after the first non-Congress government assumed office in New Delhi in 1977. The appointment of the Backward Classes Commission under B.P. Mandal in 1978 and the decision in 1990 by V.P. Singh's government to implement its recommendations marked a watershed in the country's public life. It is doubtful that the colonial administrators who introduced quotas as a way of solving their own problems of political management could have foreseen the momentous consequences their policy was to have 50 years after their departure from India.

Quotas have lodged themselves in the public consciousness in a way that might have surprised the makers of modern India. I am not talking now only of the quotas which are actually in force or even of those which are being actively contemplated, as, for instance, the quotas for women. I am talking more about the way in which many, if not most, Indians have begun to think when they deliberate on questions of equity and social justice. The management of social and political discontent through quotas has become a part of the common sense of public-spirited Indians.

About 10 years ago I wrote that our political scene was coming to resemble a checkerboard of quotas (Béteille 1998). The feeling has begun to grow that after a brief interlude, during which our leaders—Nehru, Patel, Ambedkar, Azad, and others—sought to make us into a nation of citizens, we are relapsing once again into being a society of castes and communities. The reinforcement of caste and community through identity politics does not augur well either for citizenship or for the open and secular institutions that are the backbone of civil society.

It will be unreasonable to expect identity politics to disappear from India. That is not possible or even necessary for the success of democracy. So long as the Constitution gives citizens the freedom to form associations, on no matter what basis, and so long as loyalties to language, religion, and caste remain strong in society, political leaders will use those loyalties for the mobilization of support. The issue is not of the validity of identity politics but of its scope and reach, and the limitations it imposes on public institutions designed to be governed by impersonal rules.

Apart from the great expansion in scope and scale, there are two significant differences between quotas under colonial rule and quotas today. The British not only acted with moderation, they treated quotas as a matter of policy and not of right. A whole new jurisprudence has emerged since independence to justify the adoption and expansion of quotas in every kind of institution, and they have come to be regarded as matters of right by legislators, ministers, and even judges in our country. It is impossible to continue accommodating the claims of castes and communities, including the claim for quotas in the private sector, without putting some restraints on the rights of citizenship on which so many expectations were placed just before and after independence.

The second major difference is due to a change in the nature and form of political mobilization. There was, of course, mobilization before independence, by the Indian National Congress in the cause of independence and by the Muslim League in the cause of Partition, both of which were achieved in 1947. Partly on account of the trauma of the Partition, separate claims by particular castes and communities experienced a lull for some time. As I have already pointed out, the demand for quotas acquired a new lease of life in 1990 and shows no sign of abatement. This demand has now become so insistent that no political party can oppose it in public for fear of inviting the charge of being opposed to social justice.

The Indian middle class has changed greatly in size and composition since independence. It grew in size in the early period of independence with the all-round increase in public employment, and in the last two decades with the general upturn in the economy. The steady increase in the size of the middle class has been accompanied by greater diversity in its social composition. It now accommodates persons from a much wider range of social backgrounds than it did before independence when it was much smaller in size and socially much more compact. Some of the increase in the social diversity of the middle class has been due to quotas in education and employment, but it will be a mistake to attribute all of it to quotas alone.

The middle class, as I have already indicated, is stratified in terms of wealth, occupation, education, and income, and it will be naïve to believe that the backward castes and communities are equally represented at all its levels. They are not represented in proportion to their numbers at the upper levels of professional, managerial, and administrative occupations. This has now become a major source of contention and strife in public life. It is to this that people increasingly point when they speak of India's failure to become an inclusive society. The anxiety over representation at the higher levels of education and employment tends to overshadow a much larger problem. That problem concerns the fate of the truly disadvantaged, the millions of persons who are too poor and too severely lacking in food, healthcare, and education to really count as citizens in a democratic republic.

References

Béteille, André. 1998. 'The Checkerboard of Quotas', *The Telegraph*, 24 August.

———. 2007. 'Classes and Communities', *Economic and Political Weekly*, vol. XLII, no. 11, pp. 945–52.

———. 2008. 'Constitutional Morality', *Economic and Political Weekly*, vol. XLIII, no. 40, pp. 35–42.

Bose, Nirmal Kumar. 1975. *The Structure of Hindu Society*. New Delhi: Orient Longman.

———. n.d. *Modern Bengal*. Calcutta: Vidyodaya.

Dollard, John. 1957. *Caste and Class in a Southern Town*. New York: Doubleday.

Marshall, T.H. 1977. *Class, Citizenship and Social Development*. Chicago: University of Chicago Press.

Patel, Tara (ed.). 1973. *Removal of Untouchability in Gujarat*. Ahmedabad: Gujarat University.

Chapter
8

Institutions and Networks*

I would like to discuss here two types of social arrangement which may be described as institutions and networks. The contrast between the two and their interface have figured widely—explicitly or implicitly—in social enquiry and analysis across many different domains from kinship studies to studies of economic transactions. Here my focus will be on arrangements for the pursuit of science and scholarship with special reference to the social sciences.

A major problem with contrasting institutions and networks is that they co-exist and are interwoven with each other in every human society. Although institutions have been studied extensively, they have not always been studied under that name. Many of the best insights into their nature and operation have come from the study of particular institutions such as the state, the church, or the family. Such studies do not always ask what constitutes an institution, or what different institutions have in common with each other, or what makes institutions different from other social arrangements. Institutions as well as networks have been analysed by specialists in various disciplines such as political theory, jurisprudence, history, economics, sociology, and social anthropology, and there is little uniformity in the use of terms across them.

*This text was published in *Current Science*, vol. 97, no. 2, 25 July 2009, pp. 148–56.

In the sociological literature we encounter two somewhat different conceptions of the institution: they are different, but closely related. The first is the conception of the institution as an enduring group, a kind of corporation with a definite identity. Here we see it as a system of roles and relations set in a particular social framework. In this sense we may speak of the school, the temple, or the court of law as an institution. But sociologists and social anthropologists speak not only of the school but also of education as an institution; not only of the temple (or the church) but also of a cycle of rites, whether in the temple or the home, as an institution; and not only of the court of law, but also of the judicial process as an institution. Thus, in the sociological conception, a pattern of activities is also an institution, provided it is recurrent, legitimate, and meaningful (Evans-Pritchard et al. 1954).

In what follows I shall treat institutions as systems of enduring groups rather than as patterns of recurrent activities because it is the former conception that brings out most vividly the contrast between institutions and networks. But one thing should be clear: whichever conception one favours, the deeper contrast between institutions and individuals remains. An institution has in general a different lifespan from the lifespan of the individual. Every individual goes through a process of birth, maturity, and death. Institutions too develop over time, but the two cycles of development can be easily distinguished from each other since an institution often survives without significant change the passage of individuals through it.

The sociologist Erving Goffman (1961) popularized the idea of the 'total institution', of which the boarding school is a good example. It carries to an extreme point the morphological outline and identity of the institution viewed as a system of roles and relationships. It maintains clear physical and social boundaries by which it is insulated from the outside world. Anyone who has lived in a boarding school will remember that its physical spaces are assigned social values and that many of these are 'out of bounds' to some, if not most, of its members. The regulation of space is matched by the regulation of time according to which daily, weekly, and annual cycles of activities are maintained (Thapan 1991; Béteille 2005).

Not all institutions, not even all educational institutions, have such clearly defined physical or social boundaries. The 'total institutions' to which Goffman (and Foucault) have given prominence are extreme, not to say pathological, cases, and the definition of institutions as 'organizations which *contain* people, as in the case of hospitals, prisons, mental hospitals, homes for the mentally handicapped and the like' (Wallis 1985: 399 [emphasis in original]) is tendentious. At the same time, having a definite physical location contributes a great deal to the identity of the institution, whether a family, a temple, a monastery, a college, or a court of justice.

Institutions in the sense of corporate groups are presumed to exist in perpetuity. If we take a long historical view of institutions, we will find that this is not always, or even generally, the case, that they too are subject to growth, decay, and even decease, but the presumption of perpetual existence is of considerable symbolic as well as material significance. Many institutions celebrate their anniversaries and jubilees, and when an institution is able to celebrate its centenary or even its bicentenary, the presumption of perpetual existence is reinforced.

A network, by contrast, is an individual- or ego-centred social arrangement. Each individual has his own network of social ties which expands or contracts with his passage through life. Unlike the corporate group which is presumed to exist in perpetuity, the network ceases to exist with the decease of the individual who is at its centre. Networks of interpersonal relations play an important part in the linkage of different institutions with each other. Even the most closely bounded institutions provide room for individuals to interact across their boundaries. Trade and commerce create linkages between individuals belonging to far-flung groups, and in some societies matrimonial alliances are associated with extensive networks of interpersonal relations.

Since the network is an individual-centred arrangement, in theory at least there can be as many networks in a society as there are individual members of it. In practice, there are both social and psychological constraints that act against the indefinite extension of an individual's network. Some societies allow greater latitude than others to individuals to construct networks of their choice, according to their own interest or inclination, but in no society is the scope of individual initiative in these matters unlimited.

Networks of interpersonal relations not only stretch across the boundaries of well-defined groups, they are also found within those boundaries. Human groups have formal as well as informal structures (Homans 1950). Anyone who has observed the extended family in India will know that there are informal arrangements within it whose mode of operation is often at variance with, and sometimes contrary to, the institutional structure of the family. Such networks of interpersonal relations are a common feature of every human society and co-exist with the institutionalized structure of roles and relationships. They may acquire great salience in certain spheres of activity, but they can scarcely operate effectively without the support of the established and acknowledged institutional structure.

* * *

The growth of knowledge has played an important part in the advance of human society. But the movement of knowledge is a disorderly movement. There have been for a long time small, and often dispersed, centres such as monasteries, seminaries, and colleges where individuals gathered together for the cultivation and dissemination of knowledge. In medieval times, itinerant mendicants and preachers played a part in this process. Sometimes colleges grew up and became established, as at Paris, Oxford, Cambridge, and Cairo, but their scale of operation was limited and the pace at which knowledge grew in them was slow. The aim of preserving traditional knowledge took precedence over that of creating new knowledge. Some knowledge, perhaps a large part of it, also grew outside the confines of institutions specifically established for the creation and transmission of knowledge.

This began to change from the beginning of the nineteenth century onwards. Science and scholarship came to be organized in a different way and on a different scale, and they grew at a rapidly accelerating pace. The old universities were reorganized and new ones were established throughout the world. By the beginning of the twentieth century, the establishment of universities had become an objective of state policy in most countries, and their expansion continued apace all through that century. This expansion was propelled not only by academic considerations but also by the political demand to make science and scholarship accessible to all members of society.

It is important to understand the two-fold nature of the modern university as it came to be by the middle of the last century, as a centre of learning and as a social institution. New knowledge began to grow in the nineteenth century and to spread rapidly from one country to another. The growth of new knowledge was driven in part by the economic, political, and social changes brought about by the industrial revolution, the democratic revolution, and the exploration of the world. New branches of learning began to emerge, and specialized disciplines began to differentiate themselves from the broad umbrellas of natural and moral philosophy. By the end of the nineteenth century, the universities had begun to play an important part in the formation and promotion of the various academic disciplines, first in Europe and America and then, in the course of the twentieth century, also in other parts of the world.

It tends to be forgotten that much of the intellectual ferment of the time was taking place outside the universities which were often moribund and intellectually unexciting. In the eighteenth century neither Henry Cavendish at Cambridge nor Edward Gibbon at Oxford found the university to be a particularly congenial place for serious study. They worked on their own, using their own resources. Cavendish no doubt had inherited a fortune, but it was not uncommon for a person with serious intellectual ambitions to seek out a wealthy patron and secure financial support for his work from him.

Pursuing an intellectual career outside the university continued into the nineteenth century, particularly in the humanities and social sciences. Many of those who in the nineteenth century laid the foundations for what became established academic disciplines in the twentieth century, had had their own intellectual formations outside the universities. Notable examples would be David Ricardo, John Stuart Mill, and Herbert Spencer. It is true that Karl Marx had acquired a sound intellectual formation in the University of Berlin, in his time far ahead of other universities in the world, but had very little to do with any university after he ceased to be a student. It is astonishing how much intellectual work he could do without any institutional support other than what was available at the British Museum.

Such major intellectual disciplines as sociology, anthropology, demography, social statistics, and even economics and political science as we know them today had their origins outside the universities which then came to adopt them in course of time. Like-minded scholars developed networks of interpersonal relations and formed associations devoted to the promotion of particular branches of study. With the expansion of science and scholarship, specialization became inevitable. New disciplines and new professions grew hand in hand. Professional associations and learned societies organized periodical meetings and conferences, and published journals for a readership that was becoming increasingly specialized.

The nineteenth century saw the gradual displacement of the amateur by the professional in the fields of science and scholarship. Writing at the end of that century, Émile Durkheim (1984: 2) observed, 'The time lies far behind us when philosophy constituted the sole science. It has become fragmented into a host of special disciplines, each having its purpose, method and ethos', and further, 'the functions of the scientist which formerly were almost always exercised alongside another more lucrative one, such as that of doctor, priest, magistrate or soldier, are increasingly sufficient by themselves.' Later, from his own important position as the first professor of sociology at the University of Paris, Durkheim sought to define the boundaries of the discipline so that he could act as a kind of gatekeeper for entry into the profession. By then sociology had begun to make a home for itself within the university.

The universities took time to reorganize themselves to cope with the onrush of new intellectual developments. Britain, France, and Germany followed different trajectories, but by the beginning of the twentieth century, their universities had all undergone significant transformation as both centres of learning and social institutions. The first step in the creation of a new type of university was taken with the foundation in 1810 of the University of Berlin, now known, after its main architect, as the Humboldt University.

The Humboldt University provided the blueprint for a new type of university based on the principle of 'the unity of teaching and research'. This blueprint influenced the design of many universities and was carried over into the United States with the foundation in 1875 of the Johns Hopkins University, now recognized as the first research university in the New World. Today the research university has acquired its most successful form in the United States at Harvard, Stanford, Chicago, and elsewhere.

England adopted a more gradual path of change. Its two old universities, Oxford and Cambridge, which had held the field between them for some 600 years, underwent a process of reform. Throughout the nineteenth century, new universities were created in the larger cities such as London, Manchester, Leeds, Liverpool, and Bristol, as well as in other countries in the British Empire including

Canada, Australia, and India. The new universities placed great emphasis on the examination system as a way of ensuring that their graduates had reached a certain academic standard.

France had embarked on a somewhat different course. Instead of trying to reform the existing universities, Napoleon sought to promote a set of new institutions which came to be known as the *grandes écoles* or the great schools. The *grandes écoles* are small and compact institutions with very demanding standards of scholastic achievement. They were designed to be meritocratic institutions where admission is by open national competition. In some respects they are more like our Indian Institutes of Technology (IITs) than the standard universities which are expected to cover all branches of study in the sciences and the humanities. Advancement through open competition introduced a new way of linking together careers in education and employment in accordance with Napoleon's idea of 'careers open to talent'.

The expansion of the universities since the middle of the nineteenth century took place in part in response to the expansion of knowledge in society as a whole. Once they were set up, the universities themselves took the initiative in exploring and promoting new areas of enquiry and analysis. The motto of the University of Calcutta, established in 1857, is 'Advancement of Learning'. The universities provided unprecedented scope for opening up new branches of study through collective, and not simply individual, effort that could be pursued methodically and systematically.

The shift in emphasis from introspection and speculation to empirical investigation altered the character of the universities. The change in focus and orientation and, hence, in habits of work first became manifest in the experimental sciences, and the term 'natural science' displaced the older 'natural philosophy'. By the beginning of the twentieth century the university had become the ideal setting for the kind of investigation that the scientists were conducting in association with their students, their assistants, and their colleagues. The pressure to expand the scale of work and to specialize began to come increasingly from within the institution.

As the life and work of Émile Durkheim demonstrate, the university offered an ideal setting also for work in the social sciences. It was in such a setting, first at Bordeaux and then at Paris, that he built up a team of able and dedicated scholars, which came to be named after the *Année sociologique*, the scientific periodical that he established to act as a vehicle for the publication of the new kind of research that he had initiated. Durkheim strongly advocated the view that scientific activity had to be specialized, collective, and organized in accordance with a plan. He maintained that specialization in science, as in society itself, contributed to the benefit of the whole, provided there was a proper institutional setting for the coordination of tasks that were becoming increasingly, and perhaps inevitably, differentiated. He had created such a setting for himself in the University of Paris between 1902 and 1917 (Lukes 1973).

The new disciplines, whether in the natural or the social sciences, acquired an increasingly secular cast. Theology is still taught in some contemporary universities, but it is not regarded as a modern subject in the sense in which astrophysics or plant genetics, or even sociology is. In most countries outside the Islamic world, its presence in the university is at best tolerated, and it long ceased to have the pride of place it once held in the universities of Paris and Oxford. The universities may have started as places of religious learning but in most parts of the world today they serve as places of secular study and research. This change in the focus of learning could not have come about without some change in the organization of the university as a social institution.

* * *

The nineteenth century saw the transformation of the university into a secular institution. In the older universities, such as Oxford and Cambridge, which were started on strong religious foundations, this transformation was often a slow and tortuous process. The situation is somewhat different for those that were established after the middle of the nineteenth century, which is the case with the vast majority of universities in the contemporary world. When the first universities in modern India were established at Calcutta, Bombay, and Madras in 1857, it was taken for granted that they would be secular institutions and not religious foundations. They did not have to carry with them the kind of baggage the universities set up in an earlier age had to carry into the modern world.

The modern university is a secular institution to the extent that its activities are not regulated by religious rules or religious authorities. This means that a scientist in a modern university does not have to fear incurring the censure of any religious authority in designing or conducting his experiments. It was very different in Cambridge in the seventeenth and eighteenth centuries. Accounts of Newton's life in Trinity College reveal that he performed his experiments and kept his notes in the utmost secrecy for fear of falling foul of the Church of England which maintained a strict control over his college (Keynes 1972).

The transformation of the university into a secular institution had long-term consequences for its social composition and character. So long as religion was the major focus of thought and action in it, there was reason to confine its membership to a single faith or denomination. In a Christian or a Muslim university, there could be little place for either teachers or students professing any faith other than the established one. Well into the middle of the nineteenth century, Oxford and Cambridge required adherence not only to the Christian faith generally, but specifically to the 39 Articles of the Church of England.

Such a requirement will appear anachronistic in an institution devoted to the pursuit of secular science and scholarship.

The modern university is not only mixed in the composition of its membership, but diversity in both intellectual standpoint and social background now tends to be actively pursued in it as a value. In that sense it is both a secular and an open institution. The opening of the universities to all sections of society created vast opportunities for social and economic advancement through higher education. As they opened their doors to all sections of society, more and more demands began to be made on them to contribute to the promotion of equality not only in principle but also in practice.

The admission of women has transformed the character of the university, directly as a social institution and indirectly as a centre of learning. Until virtually the end of the nineteenth century, the universities were male-dominated institutions. The traditional universities, with their close involvement in religious ideas and practices, were not designed to accommodate both men and women. The gradual incorporation of women undermined from within the cloistered character of the university and made its boundaries with the outside world more porous.

Till the middle of the nineteenth century the universities remained largely insulated from the wider society. They were meant to be hierarchical and not democratic institutions. With the advance of democracy in the twentieth century, the hierarchical model became increasingly anachronistic. The older universities in the Western countries took time to dismantle the structures of hierarchy carried over from the past, and their traces can still be seen in many of them. But it is one thing to dismantle obsolete structures of hierarchy, and quite another to install in their place new structures based on equality.

Expanding the scope for equality of opportunity became a major concern of universities in the twentieth century. The idea of equality of opportunity itself began to undergo change. At the beginning of the nineteenth century the meritarian principle appeared as a regenerative principle and many looked forward to a new social order based on Napoleon's vision of 'careers open to talent'. But by the middle of the twentieth century, John Rawls (1973: 106ff) was pointing his finger at the flaws inherent in a 'callous meritocratic society'.

What is equality of opportunity? The universities became increasingly engaged in the creation of those abilities without which, according to some, equality of opportunity would remain largely a legal fiction. Pressures to undertake their creation came both from outside, particularly the government, and from within among politically engaged students and professors. However, the passage from 'formal' to 'fair' equality of opportunity was full of unforeseen snares and pitfalls.

In what came to be known in the wake of decolonization as the 'developing' or 'less developed' countries, creating new universities and expanding existing ones became a part of the policy for all-round development. As such, the universities became directly accountable to the political establishment, including both Government and Opposition, and only indirectly to the public. The political establishment in a developing country is concerned primarily with what the universities can contribute to economic development and social equity. The maintenance and advancement of standards in teaching and research are lesser concerns. If the universities are producing more graduates from every community and class, one does not have to look too closely at how those degrees are secured and what kind of learning they are based on.

The political pressure to become socially more inclusive has led many universities to expand recklessly beyond their capacity to function effectively as centres of learning. Libraries and laboratories have languished while student admissions and faculty appointments have grown steadily. The regularity and routine of teaching and research are disregarded. Examinations are not conducted on time and the declaration of examination results is fraught with tension. Strikes, rallies, and demonstrations erupt with unfailing regularity. Unions of students, teachers, and other staff make demands that are at first ignored and then conceded under pressure. Postgraduate students are frequently absent from class and research scholars use the facilities of the university, such as its libraries, canteens, and hostels, to pursue their interest outside the university. Senior teachers use their appointments as sources of rental income.

Those who are responsible for the management of university affairs today—vice-chancellors, rectors, deans, and others—know very well that they have to sail in troubled waters. Their typical response is to create a battery of rules—statutes, ordinances, and regulations—which are ineffectual and at the same time obstructive. Many scientists and scholars have begun to feel that the mounting social and political pressures on the university have fatally undermined the possibility of sustained academic work in it. Much of what happens in the university today appears to them to be not only without legitimacy but also without meaning.

* * *

It is generally agreed that the best universities today are to be found in the United States, which has outstanding private ones such as Harvard, Stanford, and Chicago, as well as very good public ones such as the University of California at Berkeley and the University of Michigan at Ann Arbor. Yet, at a roundtable on 'Universities of the 21st Century', held at the University of Chicago in 1991 and attended by luminaries from the best American universities, the mood was elegiac rather than euphoric (*Minerva* 1992). The participants spoke about the contradictory aims and tendencies of the university, the erosion of morale in it, and the decline of academic citizenship indicated by the reluctance of its most distinguished members to take responsibility for their institution.

The modern university has evolved continuously during the last 200 years, and that evolution has not come to an end and is not likely to come to an end in the foreseeable future. Universities have grown not only in number but also in variety. The University Grants Commission publishes a list of what it calls 'University Institutions'. It includes, in addition to the universities proper, what are called 'Deemed to be Universities' and 'Institutes of National Importance'. Whereas until recently these institutions were all under the care of the Central and the state governments, there are now private universities recognized as such by the University Grants Commission.

The Indian Institute of Technology Delhi differs in many ways from the Jawaharlal Nehru University, which is its neighbour. Yet, they are both institutions established with broadly the same objectives. It is true that some of them are more orderly, more cohesive, and more purposeful than others. But they all have to work under constraints that have begun to appear burdensome to their members. One has only to spend a couple of days at an IIT to be told by both teachers and students of the plethora of rules that appear to be meaningless, obstructive, and perverse and can lead only to confusion and disorder and a decline in the commitment to the institution.

Not everyone enters an academic institution, even a premier one, from a strong commitment to the objectives of science and scholarship. But what about those—and there are many—who are genuinely committed to the vocation of science and scholarship but find existing academic institutions uncongenial because they have become at the same time inflexible and disorderly?

Today the pursuit of science and scholarship cannot be taken very far by the single individual through his own unaided effort. But he does not have to commit himself fully or even mainly to an institution with well-defined boundaries and rules of membership in order to pursue his work. The institution in the sense that I have given to the term here is not the only kind of social arrangement available to the individual for the pursuit of science and scholarship. He can pursue his objectives also through networks of interpersonal relations that cut across various institutions and disregard the boundaries between them. Networks have the advantage over institutions in being flexible and free from the kind of disorder and turmoil that have come to prevail increasingly in academic institutions.

It is my surmise that individual scholars are making increasing use of networks of various kinds. Many persons now find networks better adapted to the demands of a rapidly changing world than institutions whose adaptive capacities are constricted by bureaucratic and political pressures. Networks provide greater flexibility to individuals, but they also demand greater individual initiative. In the university, some individuals are more adept at 'networking' than others. The more adept are viewed by the less adept with a mixture of envy and scorn.

At no time was academic life confined entirely within the boundaries of the institution responsible for its care and advancement. The metaphor of the 'container' used in the context of the total institution is misleading even for the medieval university, not to speak of the modern one. The twentieth-century university was a liberal rather than a cloistered institution. As the universities expanded the scope and scale of their activities, linkages with other institutions became indispensable. Some of these linkages, as for instance representation of external members on boards and committees or appointment of external examiners, are required by the rules of the institution itself. Linkages established to meet institutional requirements provide opportunities to individuals with initiative to construct their own networks independently of the requirements of their institutions.

The proliferation of networks and their increasing use for the pursuit of science and scholarship are the outcome of various factors. I have already referred to the atrophy of innovative academic activity in many universities that is leading individuals to look for alternatives outside and across established institutions. Their search for alternatives has received an enormous stimulus from new developments in technology, particularly the technology of information and communication. The individual can now access vast, almost unlimited, quantities of information on his or her own and communicate with other individuals across the world.

The internet provides opportunities for networking that would be beyond the imagination of even the most enterprising academic 50 to 60 years ago when the worldwide expansion of university institutions began to gather momentum. Today it is possible to write a paper, submit it for publication, and read it online in published form without leaving one's home. Telephonic communication has become so inexpensive that one can easily double check on the progress of one's publication by asking the persons concerned in a different city or even a different country. The laptop and the mobile phone have become indispensable tools for many persons in professional life, and they travel with the person wherever he goes.

The internet is a relatively recent invention, and its extensive use even more recent. Its invention goes back to the mid-1970s, but it was not until the last decade of the twentieth century that its use became widespread. At first it drove a wedge in the university between those who became adept at its use and those who had to struggle to understand what it portended. This was largely a matter of generation and age. By the beginning of the present century, school children were familiar with its use while professors who had retired or were about to retire were left stranded. Soon there will be very few dinosaurs left in the academic profession without the basic skills required for using the internet.

These developments have led to changes in the work habits of academics and other professionals and in the social organization of their work. For those who are academically active and wish to remain connected with their profession, retirement does not entail the kind of break in one's activities that it generally did in the past. Until a decade or so ago, retirement from the service of the institution generally meant withdrawal from active professional work. Only a fortunate few who had achieved great success or renown were allowed to retain the privileges of institutional membership. Today there are many more possibilities for the superannuated professor to remain professionally connected.

It may well be the case that women are even more at ease than men in operating through networks of interpersonal relations. It certainly gives them greater freedom and flexibility in combining women's two roles, at home and at work (Myrdal and Klein 1956). Wherever academic work requires confinement for long periods of time in an institution away from home, women are at a disadvantage. That disadvantage is substantially reduced where they have more freedom in constructing their own networks for pursuing their work in a socially meaningful way and in settings whose choice is at least partly in their hands.

Universities and other academic institutions were designed mainly for men, and not for women and men equally: when Napoleon spoke of 'careers open to talent', he did not think of women as aspirants for those careers. Women were hardly present in university institutions till the end of the nineteenth century. Thereafter, they came into them slowly and gradually, and not without having to face resistance of many different kinds. It is perhaps no accident that their increasing participation in academic activities has come at a time when those activities are coming to be organized differently, with an enhanced role for networks, and perhaps a reduced one for institutions.

Those who are academically active today invest an increasing amount of time and energy in the organization and conduct of seminars, workshops, and conferences. These would not be successful without some financial and administrative support from one or another institution. But their real success comes from the ability to make use of networks extending far and wide across institutions. Such occasions or events provide opportunities to extend existing networks and create new ones. The time and energy available to each individual are finite, and the more actively one is engaged in extra-institutional activities, the more the obligations of academic citizenship owed specifically to one's own institution are likely to be neglected. Whether the cause of science and scholarship as a whole is advanced better by steadfast loyalty to those obligations or by operating through extensive and flexible networks of interpersonal relations is a separate question that cannot be addressed here.

Apart from access to the internet, which is now available to the academic in even the most remote university with very limited material resources, travel, including international travel, has become easier. Even in India there are now many more high-flying academics who live out of their suitcases than there were 50 years ago. Not all academic travel justifies its costs, but travel to far-flung places to participate in academic gatherings does enable individuals to establish or renew contacts with persons working on new and unfamiliar topics in their discipline or in an adjacent one.

In the 1950s and 1960s, organizing a seminar or a conference was generally the prerogative of the head of the department or institution. He might know little about the topic of the seminar or conference, but without his authorization and guiding presence, little could be done. Today an academic in even a junior position can organize or at least participate in many such gatherings at many different places if he has the drive and initiative to establish, maintain, and extend his contacts, either through face-to-face interaction or through the internet.

Interaction through conferences, seminars, and workshops at various locations affects the volume and form of academic publication. Here I may speak from personal experience only about the social sciences. Fifty years ago, one wrote less and took more time to write it. The paper had to be typed, usually by someone else, and then presented at one or two seminars before submission for publication. Today a young scholar types the paper into a personal computer and, with the click of a few buttons, circulates it to as many persons across the world as he chooses. Networking is a very important aid to the publication of what one produces.

My impression is that in disciplines such as sociology and social anthropology, fewer monographs are now published than collections of papers that originate in conferences. At many conferences one finds displays of publications, including some by reputed publishers, outside the conference room. I have been struck by the number of conference volumes among the publications on display. Not all such volumes have a long shelf life, but I am told that today, with the great advances achieved in the technology of book production, a publisher can break even and make a small profit with a print run of as few as 250 copies. The rapid expansion of networks among scientists and scholars enables science and scholarship to move a little faster.

* * *

I have in the foregoing contrasted institutions with networks, defining an institution as a corporate group with a distinct boundary that exists, or is presumed to exist, in perpetuity, and describing as a network an ego-focused or ego-centred arrangement that ceases to exist with the decease of the individual at its centre. What I would now like to stress is that institutions and networks are both social facts, although they are not social facts of the same kind.

The interpersonal relations that constitute a network are social relations. As such, they are governed by rights and obligations that are socially defined and supported by sanctions that may be legal, customary, or conventional. It is true that the individual has some freedom in deciding which network he will join and which one he will quit, but this freedom is not unlimited. An individual who is unmindful of his obligations to others, or, what is the other side of the same coin, makes too many demands on them, will find his network shrinking. Further, the individual has some choice also in entering one institution and leaving it for another. The institution may exist in perpetuity, but its individual members are, in one sense or another, transients.

The social aspects of interpersonal networks have been explored and examined from many angles by sociologists, social anthropologists, and many others. One of the founders of modern sociology, Georg Simmel (1955) was struck by the significance of networks in social life, particularly as it operated in the modern city. But their existence or significance is by no means confined to the modern urban environment. Networks operate extensively in bands and tribes whose members live by hunting, gathering, and rudimentary agriculture.

Anthropologists engaged in field studies of kinship and marriage in the simpler societies turned their attention to kinship networks in the 1940s. Starting with the study of enduring groups based on unilineal descent, they soon came to recognize the significance of the cross-cutting ties which linked distinct, and sometimes mutually hostile, descent groups with each other. The enormous significance of such cross-cutting ties was brought to light through the study of politics in stateless societies, such as the Nuer and the Tallensi in Africa (Fortes and Evans-Pritchard 1940).

Meyer Fortes published two books on the Tallensi of Ghana, bringing out the significance of both corporate descent groups and networks of interpersonal relations. He was familiar with the work of Simmel, and called his second book *The Web of Kinship among the Tallensi* (Fortes 1949). It is true that the formation of networks of kinship and marriage is not free from genealogical constraints. At the same time, genealogical proximity is only one of the factors by which the operation of such networks is governed.

Elizabeth Bott's study (1971) of family and social network was made in a very different setting in the city of London. She was interested in exploring networks of different kind and their degrees of connectedness. Husband and wife may have more or less overlapping networks, or their networks may be distinct and separate. Bott's study found that this varied significantly according to social class. In the working class, husband and wife tended to have separate networks whereas in the middle class their networks were interlinked to a greater extent. But the main difference is that in London, ties outside the domain of kinship were far more important in the creation and maintenance of networks than in Ghana.

More recently, networks have received a great deal of attention from students of economic life under advanced capitalism, particularly in the United States. There is a large and somewhat specialized literature dealing with the operation of networks in production, trade, and finance. A major focus of attention is the manner in which networks are constructed and used in order to secure economic advantage in competitive markets. Today networks are studied most actively in business schools and centres of management studies.

A turning point in the sociological study of networks was the work of Mark Granovetter (1995), acknowledged as one of the founders of the New Economic Sociology (Swedberg 2003). In a remarkable monograph based on a case study in the Boston area, Granovetter showed how individuals use contacts to further their careers. The study showed that in professional, technical, and managerial occupations, individuals used personal contacts more frequently than formal means or direct application for securing employment. Such contacts originate in diverse sources: family, neighbourhood, school, and office. Not unexpectedly, personal contacts are used more frequently for getting a job by older than by younger persons.

Granovetter's study throws doubt on the utility of a stark contrast between 'universalism' and 'particularism' in the classification of societies. The view that the use of particularistic ties is specific to traditional societies and disappears with the modernization of society is not borne out by the facts. The wheels of trade, commerce, and finance would come to a halt if they were not greased by known, reliable, and trustworthy personal contacts.

As a social arrangement, the ego-focused network, no less than the institution with a corporate identity, has a fiduciary component or a component of trust built into it. They both presuppose a universe of common values and a set of regulatory rules for their continued operation. This is readily seen in the case of the institution, but it is no less valid for the network. Interpersonal relations, with or without the envelope of an institution, cannot be sustained in the absence of trust between persons, and that, in turn, presupposes a universe of common moral values.

Networks and institutions exist in all human societies and they operate in a common medium of norms and values. It is a mistake to believe that individuals use networks only in the pursuit of self-interest whereas in institutions they act primarily in the common interest. There are free riders in institutions just as there are individuals for whom networks are nothing but instruments for the reckless pursuit of personal gain.

Interpersonal relations do not operate solely through the adjustment of interests between individuals with which those individuals and they alone are concerned. The interests of the individual are not *sui generis*: they evolve in and through social interaction. Even if the individual creates his own network, he does not create it out of nothing or put it to work in a vacuum. All economic relations, including interpersonal relations in the most dynamic of financial markets, are socially embedded. The fiduciary component in such relations is often taken for granted and ignored until there is a crisis created by the breakdown of trust. As Gordon Brown, the prime minister of the United Kingdom, pointed out at the height of the economic crisis of 2008–9, the words 'credit' and 'trust' have the same meaning, and no financial system can remain viable without them.

Institutions and networks are connected differently with each other in different domains of activity. Financial markets need banks which are institutions and without which networks, no matter how extensive their reach, cannot function. Likewise, networks among scholars and scientists require institutions such as universities and laboratories in order to do their work. Very few scientists or scholars, no matter how active they may be in creating and maintaining interpersonal networks, can operate without using the facilities available in the institutions of science and scholarship. I am not speaking now only of the benefits that secure employment in an institution provides, for the facilities available in an institution may be used also by those who are not employed in them or enjoy full membership in them. At the same time, the degree of commitment to an institution may wax or wane among its members, and that in turn will depend upon the opportunities it is possible to create in the interstices between institutions.

Some say that the university is ceasing to be an institution since more and more of its members have begun to use it as a means only and not as an end in itself. To be an institution in the proper sense of the term, a university has to be something more than a mere convenience. People who disparage the university still need it if only because it is such a great convenience. Everywhere people say that the universities are in a crisis. But this does not mean that they will become fewer in number or smaller in size. In India they are much more likely to increase in number and variety, and become larger in size. But they will also provide more scope to their more enterprising members to bypass their daily demands and create innovative arrangements for pursuing their own academic and other interests.

References

Béteille, André. 2005. 'Boarding School', in *First Proof, The Penguin Book of New Writing from India 1*, New Delhi: Penguin Books, pp. 169–200.

Bott, Elizabeth. 1971. *Family and Social Network*. New York: The Free Press.

Durkheim, Émile. 1984. *The Division of Labour in Society*. New York: The Free Press.

Evans-Pritchard, E.E. et al. 1954. *The Institutions of Primitive Society*. Oxford: Basil Blackwell.

Fortes, Meyer. 1949. *The Web of Kinship among the Tallensi*. London: Oxford University Press.

Fortes, Meyer and E.E. Evans-Pritchard (eds). 1940. *African Political Systems*. London: Oxford University Press.

Goffman, Erving. 1961. *Asylums*. Harmondsworth: Penguin Books.

Granovetter, Mark. 1995. *Getting a Job*. Chicago: University of Chicago Press.

Homans, G.C. 1950. *The Human Group*. London: Routledge and Kegan Paul.

Keynes, J.M. 1972. 'Newton, The Man', in his *Essays in Biography*, London: The Macmillan Press, pp. 363–74.

Lukes, Steven. 1973. *Émile Durkheim*. Harmondsworth: Penguin Books.

Minerva. 1992. 'The University of the Twenty-First Century; A Symposium to Celebrate the Centenary of the University of Chicago', *Minerva*, vol. XXX, no. 2, pp. 242–68.

Myrdal, Alva and Viola Klein. 1956. *Women's Two Worlds*. London: Routledge and Kegan Paul.

Rawls, John. 1973. *A Theory of Justice*. London: Oxford University Press.

Simmel, Georg. 1955. *Conflict and the Web of Group Affiliations*. Glencoe: The Free Press.

Swedberg, Richard. 2003. *Principles of Economic Sociology*. Princeton: Princeton University Press.

Thapan, Meenakshi. 1991. *Life at School*. New Delhi: Oxford University Press.

Wallis, Roy. 1985. 'Institutions', in Adam Kuper and Jessica Kuper (eds), *The Social Science Encyclopedia*, London: Routledge and Kegan Paul, pp. 391–401.

Chapter
9

Social Science Research*

My attention was struck by a caption that appeared in a daily newspaper several decades ago. It read, 'Scientists on top, not on tap'. The remark was attributed to Professor P.C. Mahalanobis and was made at the annual meeting of the Indian Science Congress in the year in which he was its general president. It was apparently provoked by a speech by Prime Minister Jawaharlal Nehru in which he exhorted scientists to be more active and diligent in the service of the nation; there may have been a hint that service to the nation amounted basically to service to the government. Professor Mahalanobis wanted to make it clear that he did not believe that scientists should be made subordinate to the government.

Should scientists be on top? I must confess that the thought that any profession or community should enjoy a unique position of pre-eminence in society makes me uneasy. At the same time, I am immediately attracted to the idea that scientists should not be on tap, that they should not be at the beck and call of the authorities in office or the funding agencies, which are often one and the same thing in

*This is a revised version of a lecture delivered on 17 August 2007 at the Indian Statistical Institute to mark the year of its platinum jubilee. I am grateful to the Institute, in whose Sociological Research Unit I began my professional career, for inviting me to deliver the lecture, and to Atis Dasgupta for his kindness and courtesy during my stay there. I am also grateful to Amita Baviskar, Mahesh Rangarajan, and Ramachandra Guha for their comments on drafts of earlier versions of the lecture.

our country. Being on tap is not only detrimental to the dignity of scientists, but it also undermines the integrity and quality of their work.

The issue is not of the superiority of scientists over others but of their autonomy in relation to the existing powers, meaning here the government of the day. Those engaged in the serious pursuit of science and scholarship have generally set a high value on their autonomy, but the conditions of autonomy and the obstacles to its maintenance have changed with changes in society and culture and in the organization of intellectual work. The constraints on intellectual work that were imposed by the church in Western countries began to ease from the beginning of the nineteenth century; but other constraints, due to the state and the market, began to make themselves increasingly felt.

Of special significance in the present context are changes in the organization of science and scholarship. In the past, scientists and scholars were able to work on their own to a far greater extent than they are able to do at present. Today most of them work in universities or other centres of advanced study and research. The autonomy of science and scholarship is thus not a matter only of the autonomy of scientists or scholars as individuals, but also of the institutions of science and scholarship within which they have to work. Individual and institutional autonomy are related to each other, but they are not one and the same thing. The autonomy of the individual scientist or scholar is not necessarily secured when his institution acquires greater autonomy, for a research institute or laboratory may be so organized that the main restraints on the freedom of individual action come from within and not outside the institution. The emphasis in this chapter will be on institutional rather than individual autonomy, although we should not lose sight of the tensions between the different claims of autonomy.

From here onwards I will focus attention on institutes of research in the social sciences. Significant differences of approach and method have developed between the different branches of science, and these have led to differences in the organization and funding of research. In all these respects, the physical and biological sciences took the lead in developing new institutional arrangements, and the social sciences have followed behind. Social science research has developed and diversified sufficiently in the last 50 years in India for it to deserve separate consideration in its own right.

I will deal in this chapter with two aspects of social science research: its content (or substance) and its organization. My view is that these two aspects are related to each other, although it is far from my intention to argue that the content of social science research is determined inexorably by the way in which it is organized. It is well to remember that many different programmes of research are pursued simultaneously and that the institutional settings in which they are pursued are themselves many and diverse. Nevertheless, there are clear affinities between the kind of research that is done and the setting in which it is done. I shall try as far as possible to make my approach to this tangled and complicated question empirical and descriptive rather than normative or prescriptive.

In a democratic country such as ours, and particularly in one where there is so much disorder in public institutions, impediments to autonomy cannot be traced to one single source. Restraints on it are rarely imposed by clear or open directives. They are more typically the consequences of rules created to promote or safeguard other objectives, some of which appear attractive enough for them to be endorsed even by those who in the end become victims of the restraints they impose on autonomy. No democratic government imposes restraints on institutional autonomy unless those restraints can be justified by an appeal to the public interest. The social scientist must ask, in each case, what the public interest is, and not take on trust what any given authority defines it to be. This task tends to be overlooked by social scientists engaged in the necessary routines of everyday research; and the more routinized the research, the more easily it is overlooked.

Restraints on the autonomy of the institutions of science and scholarship cannot be effectively maintained without the complicity of individual scientists and scholars. This makes it extremely difficult to remove them, or even to discuss them openly. The complicity need not be premeditated, and it is by no means always motivated by considerations of material gain, although such considerations cannot be ruled out in principle.

* * *

Social science research began to acquire a new institutional profile in India after the country became independent. Until then, such research as was done was done mainly in the universities or by persons from the universities, usually economists, who conducted enquiries into specific problems on behalf of the government. The institutional base of research broadened and became diversified after independence. Today a great deal of research, of variable quality, is done outside the universities.

Before independence, the Indian universities were few in number and their postgraduate departments were small in size. Although there were notable exceptions, not much research in the social sciences was done in those departments. Most postgraduate departments concentrated on teaching rather than research. They admitted research students, but, at least in the humanities and social sciences, there were hardly any PhD programmes worth the name. A notable exception was the department of sociology in the University of Bombay which, under G.S. Ghurye, produced a steady stream of PhDs. This research was started before the days of development planning, and it had little direct connection with economic or social policy. Its value lay in the contribution it made to a deeper understanding of the changing Indian reality.

There was very little separate funding for research within the universities and little research of long-term value was done outside them. While money for research was lacking in the universities, the government was prepared to make money available for research that related to its own concerns. The scope for planning and policymaking within the government expanded enormously after independence. By the middle of the twentieth century, governments, particularly in democratic countries, had begun to recognize that policymaking in economic and social matters benefited from being informed by systematic research. The first prime minister of independent India, Jawaharlal Nehru, was particularly attentive to the requirements of research for informed policymaking.

It does not take much sociological acumen to see that the perceptions of the government and of the profession are not likely to be identical on the priorities of research, its relevance, its scale, its costs, and its time frame. Administrators, who often pride themselves on their practical knowledge of economic and social matters, are likely to be impatient with work that they regard as of 'purely academic' interest. Social scientists, in their turn, are likely to regard bureaucrats as short-sighted and narrow-minded, and without a broader and deeper understanding of social and economic matters. In my experience, officials of the government have an eye for what I call 'immediate-return' research whereas social scientists, as professionals, have also a commitment to 'delayed-return' research.

The independence of India provided opportunities not only for the expansion of research but also for the creation of new institutions. Most of the major institutes of social science research came up in the wake of India's independence. The Indian Statistical Institute was established in advance of independence, but its real expansion and consolidation as a major institution of national and international importance came after 1947.

An institution for advanced study and research that was created with the independence of India very much in mind was the Delhi School of Economics, with which I have had a life-long association. The Delhi School of Economics and the Indian Statistical Institute were established with somewhat different objectives in view. But their founders were both men of outstanding ability and vision. And they were both deeply committed to the regeneration of the nation as well as the autonomy of the institutions of science and scholarship. What I have learnt from their examples is that the autonomy of such institutions is an essential condition for the health and well-being of a democratic society.

Dr V.K.R.V. Rao never tired of explaining, on both public and private occasions, the reasons that led him to establish the Delhi School of Economics. As a leading economist, he had provided advice to the government on technical matters both before and after independence. He had acquired knowledge and experience of the kind of enquiry and investigation that the government conducted through its own agencies. He would be the first to acknowledge that such research was necessary and desirable. But he would also insist that in a free country it was not sufficient. No matter how well the government performed, its performance had to be assessed by institutions that could review its work with critical detachment from the outside. The prevalent view in the Delhi School of Economics in the 1950s and 1960s was that the social scientist had an obligation to serve the nation and that he could do so not by sacrificing his autonomy but by safeguarding it.

Those who laid the foundations for social science research in independent India recognized the need to mobilize and organize resources on a larger scale than had been done in the past. By resources I mean not just material or financial resources but also intellectual ones. In India it has proved difficult to create and sustain institutions that serve a public purpose and also maintain their autonomy. This is largely because of a widespread, though generally unstated, belief that the government, and the government alone, knows what the public purpose is, and therefore all public institutions must not only be accountable to the government but in the end also be regulated by its functionaries.

* * *

Research in the social sciences acquired a new direction and a new impetus after independence from the national concern with development. Social science and social policy came to be more closely linked than they had been in the past. The Government of India, which placed development very high on its agenda of priorities, took a special interest in the kind of social science research that might contribute to the solution of the problems it viewed as most urgent. Among the social sciences, some disciplines benefited more than others from the ready availability of government support for research in the cause of development.

In the years immediately following independence, many able social scientists turned to development studies. Although the problem of development raised important conceptual and theoretical questions, policy considerations were uppermost in the research in which they became engaged. The fact that funding was more readily available for research directed to the ends of policy no doubt added to its attraction.

It is far from my intention to suggest that in the 1950s and 1960s social scientists were attracted to the study of development simply because funding was easily available for research in that field. They were attracted to it because the problems of development appeared intellectually, and not just politically, challenging. It is difficult to recapture the intellectual excitement created by the problem of development in a country that had remained backward and stagnant for generations but had at last come into its own with the attainment of national independence. There was also considerable international interest in India's prospects for development. The Indian experiment was viewed by many as a test case from which other countries might benefit. Social scientists from many parts of the world came to India to observe and analyse the development process with a special interest in its policy aspects.

Not only the Government of India but international agencies and foundations, such as the Ford Foundation, came forward with offers of support. Some of these agencies are likely to have thought that a good way of influencing policy in the 'new nations' was by supporting research on development. Development studies emerged and established itself as a new and expanding field of enquiry and investigation. Although institutes and centres for development studies came up also in some of the advanced industrial countries, it was understood that the research done there would have the underdeveloped or less developed countries as its focus. Along with development studies came development cooperation between the developed and the developing countries, and development aid from the former to the latter.

Economists were at the forefront of the new initiative in social science research. The subject of development studies was in a sense their creation. At first when people spoke of development, they generally meant economic development. Attention was soon extended to political development and even social development, although social and cultural anthropologists were always a little sceptical about the concept of social development. Economic science already enjoyed a pre-eminent position among the social sciences and this pre-eminence became securely established when development studies came to dominate social science research. Among all the social sciences, economics was considered to be the most precise and the most practical, and therefore of most value to the government, and particularly to a government that was committed to centralized planning. The perception among planners and policymakers in the government was that economics was a policy science in a way in which sociology or social anthropology, or even political science, was not. If in the early years of development planning the government were to turn for advice to any social scientist, it would generally be to an economist.

At the time of independence, India was widely perceived to be a backward country, and backwardness was viewed essentially in economic terms. The leaders of newly independent India acknowledged its backwardness but attributed it mainly to the long years of colonial rule. India had adopted a democratic political order, and that was put on the credit side. But the stigma of backwardness remained. Efforts were made from the start to remove or at least reduce poverty and economic stagnation, but for decades the country remained stuck with a very low rate of economic growth, which came to be dubbed as the 'Hindu rate of growth', a term attributed to the economist Raj Krishna who became my colleague at the Delhi School of Economics.

A new kind of division of the world emerged in the wake of decolonization in the middle of the twentieth century. This was based on the distinction between the economically backward and the economically advanced countries. The economically backward countries came to be designated as the Third World. The countries of the Third World, in Asia, Africa, and Latin America, differed greatly among themselves historically, culturally, and socially. What they had in common was that they were all economically backward. The terminology changed from 'backward' to 'underdeveloped', then to 'less developed' and, finally, to 'developing', but the perception of a basic and fundamental deficiency in their economy and society remained and became deeply entrenched.

It is not that poverty and economic stagnation were the only problems that confronted Indians in the wake of independence. There was a plethora of social and political problems that faced the country as it struggled to overcome the trauma of Partition. However, it was the economic problem that appeared most amenable to treatment by research-based policies. It will be hardly an exaggeration to say that India's first prime minister was a votary of the scientific method, and he gave his ear more readily to economists than to other social scientists. And the economists had convinced themselves and others that the root of every social problem in India lay in its economic backwardness. One reason why economic growth attracted the attention of planners, policymakers, and many others lay in the belief that unlike, say, secularization or social integration, it could be measured reliably and accurately.

In my recollection of the Delhi School of Economics in the 1950s and 1960s, growth and development overshadowed all other topics of discussion among the economists. I have in mind not only those like Dr V.K.R.V. Rao who joined the government in the early 1960s, but also others such as K.N. Raj (2006) and Amartya Sen (1970). No matter what the economists discussed, whether it was trade, industry, agriculture, labour, or capital, the discussion never strayed far from the context of growth. For many of them, economic analysis would amount to very little if it did not contribute to economic policy. All of this left me a little uneasy because, at least at that time, I did not feel that sociology showed itself at its best as a policy science (Béteille 1972).

It was soon realized by economists as well as others that growth in the crude material sense of an increase in the gross national product or per capita income could not by itself serve as a satisfactory indicator of a country's advance. An increase in the rate of growth might have an adverse effect on the pattern of distribution, widening the gap between the rich and the poor. Very soon the concept of development, which sought a more rounded view, emerged as an attractive alternative to that of growth. Social scientists are now more inclined to speak of development than of growth. However, it must be realized that growth in the sense of a measurable increase in the gross national product remains at the core of the concept of development as it is employed in social science research. Growth may not be a sufficient condition of development but it is still a necessary condition of it in the thinking of social scientists in general.

Those concerned with growth and development have always been aware of the problems of inequality. It has been a matter of common knowledge among economists that in the early stages of growth, economic inequality increased instead of declining in what are now the advanced industrial countries. Hence, measures to balance growth with equity have been an important consideration in both development research and development policy (Tendulkar 1983).

In a country like India it is difficult for the policymaker, the social scientist, and even the ordinary citizen to keep his attention away from inequality for long because its marks are present everywhere. Nor is inequality simply a matter of the distribution of income among individuals or households. There are vast social disparities between castes and communities that are rooted in a hierarchical structure based on custom and usage. Not all social disparities are as easy to measure as the inequalities of income. Nor are those that are most easy to measure always the most significant ones. The problem with inequality is that it is hydra-headed. It does not advance or retreat all at once. As old forms of it decline, new forms begin to reveal themselves.

Rapid economic growth has unintended and unwanted consequences that can be anticipated, at least to some extent, by systematic research. Again, these consequences are not all equally easy to measure, but with patience and care they can be analysed in a systematic way. India had been seen by many as a land of stable and self-sufficient communities. Nowhere in the world has economic growth left the social life of the community untouched. Often it has had very disruptive consequences on it.

The social costs of economic growth could not be left only to the economists to analyse and assess. The field of development studies had to expand in order to accommodate other social scientists such as sociologists, social anthropologists, political scientists, geographers, and even historians. Not all social science disciplines are equally well equipped to address the problems of growth and development. The basic concerns of several of them are related only indirectly to those problems, no matter how broadly we define them. Some of the practitioners of these other disciplines trimmed their sails to the prevailing winds to enter the stream of development research. To what extent the singular attraction of development studies has impeded the free flow of research initiatives into such fields as family, kinship, religion, local-level politics, and social mobility is not easy to determine.

* * *

The government of independent India showed its interest in expanding the facilities for advanced study and research from the very beginning. A number of new universities were started and centres of advanced study in a variety of disciplines were set up in the universities at the initiative of the University Grants Commission. There were specialized research institutes outside the university system that also began to attract the attention of the government. The government, which was already providing grants-in-aid to such institutes in the natural sciences, began to consider extending support to institutes in the social sciences.

The fledgling research institutes in the social sciences required grants-in-aid from the government for their sustenance. The Government of India set about creating an institutional mechanism through which grants-in-aid could be provided on a regular and sustained basis for social science research. In doing so, it took into account the fact that a mechanism had already been created for the benefit of research in the natural sciences. The Indian Council of Social Science Research (ICSSR) was created in 1968 and registered in 1969.

Autonomy was a concern at the very foundation of the Council. The prime mover in its foundation was Dr Rao who had been earlier instrumental in the establishment of the Institute of Economic Growth and the Delhi School of Economics and was then the minister for education in the Union cabinet. The Council was not set up within the government but as a registered society under the Societies Act of 1860, with its own Memorandum of Association. However, the appearance of autonomy conceals many ambiguities in its actual structure and functioning. It has become clear through these ambiguities that autonomy means different things to different persons. There are differences between officials and professionals regarding what autonomy in public institutions should mean, and these differences have become increasingly apparent with the passage of time. Many professional social scientists outside the government have begun to feel that the autonomy of the Council is nominal, if not notional.

Shortly after its creation, the Council brought within its ambit a number of research institutes that were already in existence or came up soon afterwards. These included the Institute of Economic Growth and the Centre for the Study of Developing Societies in Delhi, the A.N. Sinha Institute in Patna, the Gandhian Institute in Varanasi, and the Centre for Studies in the Social Sciences in Kolkata. Two things that the government seemed to be mindful about were the quality and excellence of research, and the autonomy of the institute where such research was to be undertaken. Its interest in autonomy is signalled by the fact that the Government of India's Resolution of 18 March 1971 laid down that the institute should be 'registered under the Societies Act of 1860 or as a Public Trust'. As I have just pointed out, the Council itself was set up under the same Act so that there was at least the intention to maintain a congruence between it and the research institutes under its care.

New research institutes began to emerge from around 1970 onwards. The presence of the ICSSR no doubt acted as an incentive for their growth. It was, or appeared to be, a munificent source of research funds where until it was set up, very little money was available for social science research. In the early years of its existence the Council played a proactive role in the creation of new research institutes in the different parts of the country. The general idea was to have at least one research institute in every state. Except for the ones in Delhi, the others are funded partly by the Union government and partly by the governments of the states in which they are located. There are at present 27 such research institutes under the care of the ICSSR.

The institutes just referred to are not the only places in which research in the social sciences is done today. Some of it is done in the university departments, including research on projects and fellowships funded by the ICSSR. Research of high quality continues to be done in the best university departments such as those at the Delhi School of Economics and the Jawaharlal Nehru University. At the same time, many postgraduate departments in the universities are now languishing, and the centres of advanced study have not all lived up to their promise. There has been some migration of talent from the universities, which are often large and disorderly places, to the institutes of research, and it has been argued that the de facto separation of teaching and research to which this has contributed has been detrimental to both.

The scope of social science research has changed considerably from the middle of the twentieth to the beginning of the twenty-first century. This is not simply because of changes in economy, polity, and society, but also because of advances in concepts, methods, and theories in the last 50 to 60 years. As I have indicated, the research institutes that came up in the early decades of independence reflected the dominant policy concerns of the Union and state governments, which, at that time, were with growth and development. These also were the major research concerns of the social scientists who gave shape and direction to those institutes at their foundation.

The preoccupation with growth and development may be seen in the very names of the institutes to which I have been referring: Institute of Economic Growth (Delhi), Centre for the Study of Developing Societies (Delhi), Institute of Development Studies (Jaipur), Madras Institute of Development Studies (Chennai), Centre for Development Studies (Thiruvananthapuram), and so on. It is true that new topics of research have been taken on board in several of the institutes, but growth and development provide the running thread for most of the research undertaken there. Even if individual researchers want to explore other, unrelated fields, the funding agencies try to ensure that they do not stray too far from the field of development research, which they believe to be the one which yields the best fruits from the policy point of view.

I would like to emphasize that many of these institutes have undertaken valuable research in a variety of different fields. In addition to economists, they have accommodated sociologists, anthropologists, political scientists, psychologists, and others, including some of the best in the country. But the fact remains that their dominant research concerns have been with development and that, with the notable exception of a few institutes, economists have been more prominent in them than other social scientists.

Perhaps the time has come to ask if having a fixed framework of research based on the idea of development may not become an encumbrance in the future, or, even, if it is not already becoming one. It was natural at the time of independence for the advanced industrial countries to think of India as a backward or underdeveloped country. It may have also been natural for Indian social scientists to regard the problems of growth and development as the ones that needed their most urgent attention at that time. The country sought and received development aid, including aid for development research. But the times have begun to change. India is no longer caged in the Hindu rate of growth, and we are ceasing to be regarded as a backward or underdeveloped country. In order to look for new horizons of social science research in India, it may be necessary for us to put the straitjacket of development studies behind us.

I should make it clear that I do not for a moment believe that the enhanced pace of growth in the Indian economy and the many changes that have taken place and are taking place in it have led to the disappearance of poverty, hunger, disease, ill-health, and inequality from the country. These are not only a part of the Indian reality, but they need continuous and systematic study by social scientists. But it is difficult to see why these important features of any large and complex society have to be fitted into the framework of development studies in the case of India. There are outstanding studies of poverty and inequality by social scientists in the advanced industrial societies (Townsend 1979; Wilson 1987). These studies have been conducted for the most part by social scientists who would scarcely be regarded as experts in development studies.

Having provided a new direction to social science research in India, the framework of development studies acquired a life of its own. It began to influence research on topics that could do just as well, if not better, outside its ambit. The real problem with the framework of development studies is that it is based on the presumption of a dichotomous division of the world into countries that are advanced and those that are backward, or between developed and underdeveloped countries. I do not know any strong advocate of development studies who does not carry somewhere in his mind a dichotomous view of the world as being divided into backward and advanced countries. Such a view is misleading and it is an impediment to the free growth of comparative studies (Béteille 2002: 72–133).

* * *

Should there be a fixed agenda for social science research under conditions of continuous changes in economy, polity, and society? Should there be a single agenda for social science research in a country as large and diverse as India? I would like to pursue a little further the argument that restraints on institutional autonomy act against flexibility and innovation in social science research.

As I have indicated, some research in the social sciences was done mainly in the universities even before independence. But, with the exception of a few economists, social scientists did not have much say in policymaking. It is true that social anthropologists such as J.H. Hutton and T.C. Hodson played some part in the shaping of official policy, but they did so as members of the Indian Civil Service rather than as anthropologists.

Things changed with the attainment of independence. The Indian intelligentsia had radically new expectations of a state of their own which they could not have had of a colonial state. Many took it for granted that the government should take charge of the commanding heights not only of the economic system but also of the system of knowledge. It was in those years easy to believe in the benevolent intentions of a government headed by Jawaharlal Nehru and including so many of the leaders of the nationalist movement. Social scientists were yet to learn that the urge to impose restraints on the autonomy of research is a characteristic of all bureaucracies and not simply of those serving a colonial state. The hope that the bureaucratic urge to impose restraints on the autonomy of academic institutions would disappear with the passage from colonial dependence to national independence proved to be illusory.

Nehru, more than any other national leader, genuinely believed in the positive contribution of science and scholarship to the regeneration of the nation. He put his trust in both natural and social scientists, and they in turn had abundant faith in him. He did his best to convince scientists of every description that the Government of India was on their side. When in the early years of independence, scientists working in a range of disciplines—physicists, biologists, economists, and others—reached out to the government, they did not do so only or mainly for opportunistic reasons but because many of them genuinely believed that that was the best way to serve the country—and to serve science.

It was largely in this spirit that the ICSSR was conceived and brought into being. Those who were responsible for giving shape to it were inspired by the Nehruvian vision of the role of science in the regeneration of society, although by the time it came into being, Nehru himself had left the scene. The original impulse for its creation came from Dr V.K.R.V. Rao, who was then the minister of education in the Union government, and its first chairman was Professor D.R. Gadgil, then the deputy chairman of the Planning Commission. Both Rao and Gadgil were public-spirited economists of the highest professional standing, and they both set a high value on the autonomy of the institutions of science and scholarship.

There can be little doubt that the ICSSR in its initial years played a very fruitful role in the promotion of social science research. It made funds for research available on a larger scale than ever before. It also created a sense of the importance of social science research in the formulation of policy and in the appraisal of its results. It encouraged the entry of young social scientists into research and opened up opportunities for social science research outside the major metropolitan centres in the country.

Somewhere down the line, the energy and enthusiasm for social science research that the ICSSR had generated in its early phase dissipated. Too much was invested in a particular kind of research directed to policies of a particular kind. Development studies, which had provided so much intellectual stimulation to so many young social scientists in the 1960s and the 1970s, gradually ran out of steam. The confidence in the government's capacity to transform economy and society wore thin, and with it the confidence in the kind of research the government was eager to support.

The attempt to infuse new life into development studies by introducing the idea of 'development alternatives' or 'alternatives in development' made it a little easier to accommodate research by non-economists. But it did not really rescue development research from the routinization of project work that had begun to set in. The Union and the state governments seemed to be comfortable with the routinization and had little incentive to disturb the established agenda of research.

As I have pointed out more than once, the social scientists who took the lead in creating the ICSSR were forthright in their support for autonomy. However, autonomy has many different aspects, which makes it difficult to provide a definition of it that will be acceptable to all. Suffice it to say that autonomy is easy to advocate in principle but difficult to safeguard in practice. Being an academic, I know only too well that university professors are given to making extravagant claims for autonomy that they themselves do not always accept literally; and there are academic grandees who want autonomy for the institutes they have created but not for their own junior colleagues.

A certain amount of autonomy is conceded by all parties and taken for granted in the institutions of science and scholarship in India. Even when the government provides all the funding, as it does for the ICSSR, it does not dictate the findings of research. Once approval is given for a particular project, there is little interference with the course of research or the conclusions to which it leads. Professional opinion is sufficiently well developed and alert in India for the government to be able to do this openly and directly without adopting draconian measures and discrediting itself with the press and the public. But where it holds the purse strings, it can exercise its influence on the priorities of research by regulating the flow of patronage. Political and bureaucratic influence on public institutions, including the institutions of science and scholarship, is exercised not by issuing direct commands but through the distribution and redistribution of patronage among individuals and institutions dependent on the government for funds.

Who should determine the agenda of research and its priorities? Where research is driven mainly by considerations of policy and also funded by the government, it is natural for the officials of the government to feel that they should have a say in the selection of the topics of research if not in the evaluation of its results. It is well to remember that the Indian Administrative Service is a body of well-qualified persons. Some of its members have had experience of research from within and have secured PhD degrees from Indian and even foreign universities. It is much easier for a serving officer to take a few years off in mid-career and secure a PhD degree in sociology, political science, or public administration than to secure one in physics or biology. At the same time, it is important to keep in mind the distinction between a social scientist by qualification and one by profession.

The agenda of development studies had, as I have pointed out, a wide appeal in the early decades of independence in the government as well as the profession. An agenda which acquires an appeal of that kind tends to develop a life of its own and to continue on its course through inertia. In my experience, civil servants tend to be governed by inertia even more than academics in universities and research institutes. Officials exercise their influence on the agenda of research when they are able to decide who will represent the profession in such important bodies as the ICSSR. In a large and diverse country such as ours, it is never very difficult to find scientists and scholars whose thinking harmonizes with the thinking in the government.

The founders of the ICSSR acted on the basis of mutual trust between the government and the profession. Some of them, such as V.K.R.V. Rao and D.R. Gadgil, held important positions in the government at the time. They took it for granted that the autonomy of the social scientists would be respected, but they left the main part of the control of the Council in the hands of the government. It would have been difficult for them to foresee either the radical changes of the last two decades in the operation of the government or the great expansion and diversification of the profession, itself associated to some extent with the creation of the ICSSR.

In the context of autonomy and control, the most striking feature of the Council is its composition. Since its very inception it has been composed entirely of nominees of the Government of India, with the sole exception of the Member-Secretary, in whose appointment the Council was given some say. This kind of structure and composition can be understood if we go back to the conditions under which the ICSSR was established. The conditions have changed, and what may have been appropriate once now appears anachronistic. A body which is composed entirely of nominees of the government may sustain the spirit of autonomy for some time, but sooner or later it is bound to act as a creature of the government.

* * *

Having stressed the value of autonomy in the institutions of science and scholarship, let me say that autonomy cannot be absolute or unconfined, particularly in a public institution dependent largely, if not entirely, on external funding. Funding apart, no institution can stand on its own, in complete isolation from everything else. Every institution depends, in one way or another, on other institutions and on the wider society by which it is sustained.

An autonomous institution is one which is governed by rules formulated and protected by its own members. These rules must conform to the objectives for which the institution exists and to the legal order of the society of which it is a part. The rules of an institution include the rules by which its members are inducted, and an institution is autonomous to the extent that its existing members have a voice in the induction of new members. An institution whose members are selected by an external agency in ways that remain obscure to its past and present members cannot be considered autonomous in the accepted sense of the term.

The relationship between a public institution and the outside world is never free from tension. Those within the institution ask for greater autonomy and those outside it for greater accountability. What is clear and evident is that an institution of science and scholarship, whether a university or a research institute or council, cannot use the plea of autonomy to assert that it is accountable only to its own members. Many such institutions grossly misuse the resources at their disposal and they must be held to account for flagrant and persistent violations of their own norms of conduct. Wastage and misuse of resources are endemic in our public institutions. But then, autonomous and semi-autonomous institutions are not the only ones in which they occur: the ministries and departments of the government are themselves scarcely free from the common practice.

The question is not whether an institution of science and scholarship should be accountable, but by what kind of agency and in what manner it should be called to account. The conventional wisdom is that the authority to which it must answer for its conduct should be the one from which it receives its funding. This conventional wisdom has to be questioned and seriously scrutinized.

Funding agencies are of different kinds, each with its own demands of conformity to its particular tests and measures of accountability. In India, money for social science research comes mainly from government rather than business or industry. The convention of terminology which equates government with the 'public' and business with the 'private' sector can be misleading. The magic of the word 'public' lulls people into the belief that public control of institutions is open and transparent whereas, in fact, control by officials of the government is often the opposite of being either open or transparent.

It is undeniable that the ministries and departments of the government perform important public functions and discharge important public responsibilities: only an anarchist will deny to the state any significant role in the regulation of public affairs. But it is doubtful that the government can be regarded as the pre-eminent custodian and protector of the public interest in every sphere of activity. Government functionaries do not always have the knowledge and understanding needed to decide what kinds of programmes research institutes should adopt in their own long-term interest or even what kinds of rules serve best the requirements of their internal regulation.

Not all institutions of science and scholarship are equally open to intrusion that may be justified by the argument for accountability. The less technical their work and the closer it is to current affairs and to immediate policy concerns, the more open they are to such intrusion. There is a difference here between the natural sciences and the social sciences. In my experience, high officials who control the purse strings are more cautious and circumspect in their views on priorities of research in particle physics or molecular biology than on research in sociology, political science, or economics. Many of them have definite views on what kind of research they consider to be relevant for the betterment of economy, society, and policy. The fact that such views are often expressed confidently does not mean that they go very deep. If such persons have similar views on the natural sciences, they do not express them openly.

Research in the social sciences, particularly in such disciplines as sociology and political science, is undeniably closer to common sense and current affairs than research in the natural sciences. But this does not mean that the formulation of the problem of enquiry; the choice of concepts, methods, and data; or the assessment of the time and the material and human resources required for the work can be undertaken by anyone with a strong dose of common sense and close experience of financial and administrative matters. Persons with such experience may be given a say in the funding and organization of research, but they cannot be given the final say.

Public scrutiny and appraisal of the institutions of science and scholarship is essential for their own health and well-being and not simply to ensure that public funds are not misused. Such scrutiny and appraisal should be undertaken periodically by independent committees in which the professions such as law, medicine, literature, the arts, and the sciences are represented. There is far too little review and appraisal of the work of the institutions of science and scholarship by independent committees, and this has not been conducive to the emergence of new initiatives in their work. This is not likely to happen without some loosening of the government's stranglehold over institutions that were designed for autonomy and continue to be designated as autonomous.

The social sciences in India need to break free from an agenda of research of which the main concerns are the policy concerns of the government. In doing so they will not be acting against the public interest but redefining it in broader terms. They should be the first to recognize that while they may have some obligation of service to the government, that is not the same thing as service to the nation or to society as a whole. Informed and intelligent policy is no doubt important in giving direction to change, and social scientists should do what they can to help in the formulation and implementation of such policy. But it will be naïve to believe that a society changes simply because the government decides to change it in certain ways. There are other forces and factors, besides the policies of the government, that operate at a deeper level and whose consequences are not easy to foresee. These need to be studied by social scientists on a long-term basis, away from the distractions of immediate policy concerns.

Every society accumulates its own stock of intellectual capital by which its members are sustained no less than by the material resources available to them. Systematic knowledge of the economy, polity, and society is an important component of this intellectual capital. It is indispensable for policymaking and policy appraisal, but its value extends far beyond its usefulness to policymakers. Informed choices have to be made by all citizens—teachers, housewives, voters, and others—and not simply by those in authority. In the modern world, systematic knowledge is of vital importance to a civilized way of living. The value of social science research lies not simply in its contribution to policymaking, but, in a broader and more fundamental sense, also in what it contributes to the making of an informed citizenry.

In a democratic social and political order, public consciousness and public opinion should be at least as important as government policy in bringing about change. We cannot, in a country of the size and diversity of India, think of public opinion as a single, homogeneous medium. No doubt each individual knows something of the operation of economic and political processes, of family, kinship and religion, and of caste and class in his own particular environment. But this knowledge is generally both limited and biased. Research in the social sciences helps in advancing our knowledge of the social world in which we live and making it wider and deeper.

The processes through which the findings of research enter the public consciousness are slow and tortuous, and they operate unevenly across the different segments and strata of society. Yet the long-term value of such findings for society as a whole cannot be gainsaid. To take an obvious example, the writing of school textbooks in India leaves much to be desired and can benefit greatly from a wider use of the findings of social science research. A wider acquaintance with those findings can also help newspaper writing to become less superficial and more rigorous. For these things to happen, social science research must free itself from its immoderate dependence on the requirements of policymaking in the government.

India is a very large country with a numerous and growing body of social scientists. There will be enough able and competent persons among them to continue to undertake the kind of research on problems of development in which the government has a legitimate interest. But the great days of development research lie in the past and not the future. My sense is that the new directions in social science research will not emerge within the field of development studies but outside it.

As I have emphasized, development studies provided a great stimulus to social science research in the early decades of independence. But it also created and reinforced our image of India as a less developed country, or an LDC, and one that was fated to remain in that condition for as long as one could see. When that image changes, as it is bound to sooner or later, the appeal of development research will be diminished. However, one should not underestimate the inertia of established habits of work among social scientists or established habits of thought within the government.

References

Béteille, André. 1972. 'The Social Sciences: The Problem', *Seminar*, no. 157, pp. 10–14.

———. 2002. *Sociology*. New Delhi: Oxford University Press.

Raj, K.N. 2006. *Inclusive Growth* (edited by Ashoka Mody). Mumbai: Orient Longman.

Sen, Amartya (ed.). 1970. *Growth Economics*. Harmondsworth: Penguin Books.

Tendulkar, Suresh D. 1983. 'Economic Inequality in an Indian Perspective', in André Béteille (ed.), *Equality and Inequality*, New Delhi: Oxford University Press, pp. 71–128.

Townsend, Peter. 1979. *Poverty in the United Kingdom*. Harmondsworth: Penguin Books.

Wilson, William J. 1987. *The Truly Disadvantaged*. Chicago: University of Chicago Press.

Chapter
10

Social Theory and Social Policy*

Those who pass through institutions of higher education do not need to be reminded that they have been in a privileged place. Only a miniscule minority of young men and women are able to find places in universities and other centres of higher learning. Certainly, merit and ability are important in securing admission to such institutions, but luck also plays some part. I speak not only of the luck that contributes to individual success in examinations, but also of the luck of being born in a home that has the resources to provide a good elementary and secondary education to its children. One must, of course, make the best use of the opportunities one has, but it will be wrong to forget that there are millions of others to whom those opportunities never came.

In a memorable convocation address delivered at Allahabad just after India's independence, Jawaharlal Nehru had said that a university stands for 'the adventure of ideas, and for the search for the truth'. Our universities have failed to live up to Nehru's image of them, and they have much to answer for. Many of them reflect, and some even magnify, the confusion and disorder prevalent in the wider society. Yet, there are—and I hope there will continue to be—islands of excellence in which the pursuit of ideas is valued for its own sake.

*This is the text of the convocation address delivered at the Tata Institute of Social Sciences, Bombay in 2001.

In an institution of higher learning, the mind is trained to examine problems calmly, dispassionately, and in a disciplined manner. I cannot emphasize too strongly the value of a disciplined mind in a world marked by confusion and disorder. It is said that our social problems are of such magnitude that sentiment, sympathy, and concern rather than disciplined analysis should guide us in our approach to them. Certainly, social problems cannot be seriously addressed where there is an absence of sympathy and fellow feeling. But good intentions alone do not solve social problems, or any kind of problem. What is striking about our public life today is the abundant and copious expression of good intentions that lead to little or no fruitful action.

At any rate, in a premier institution of higher learning, one should not feel embarrassed to make the case for clear and dispassionate analysis as a condition for both understanding and action. A famous revolutionary text declared, 'The philosophers have only interpreted the world, in various ways; the point is to change it.' The world cannot be changed without a clear understanding of its existing constraints and the choices available under those constraints. Ill-conceived programmes of change, even where impelled by the best of intentions, tend to bear bitter, and sometimes poisonous, fruit.

* * *

The outside world that awaits the graduates of today is in many ways different from the one they have largely inhabited as students. Its landmarks are uncertain and unclear. Good intentions will not be enough in negotiating those landmarks. A reasoned understanding of the wider society and the changes taking place in it will help them at least to see where they stand. It is here that a training in social theory is of value, for it teaches us to face the contradictions of the real world with clear eyes.

Among the many contradictions that are a part of the contemporary Indian reality, I would like to single out for brief attention what may be called the contradictions of equality. On the eve of India's independence, Jawaharlal Nehru had written, 'The spirit of the age is in favour of equality, though practice denies it almost everywhere'. Being an optimist, he had gone on to add, 'Yet the spirit of the age will triumph' (Nehru 1961). More than 50 years after independence we can plainly see that the spirit of the age has not triumphed, at least not in the sense in which or to the extent to which Nehru and his generation had hoped. A common tendency in the face of this is to put the blame for it on some particular members or sections of society: politicians, bureaucrats, capitalists, or some other easy target of verbal attack. Yet, it is obvious from the viewpoint of social theory that no single class or section of society, no matter how malign, can be held solely responsible for so pervasive and deep-rooted a phenomenon as social inequality. By being self-consciously virtuous we obscure from our own view the many different sources from which inequality draws its sustenance in our society as well as in other societies.

Here I would like to draw attention to an observation made by the French sociologist Raymond Aron. For him, a characteristic feature of modern societies is that they are 'both egalitarian in aspiration and hierarchical in organization' (Aron 1968). He was drawing attention to the fact that however strongly we might desire equality, or say that we desire it, some forms of inequality are inescapable. For instance, if we want equality of opportunity, we must be prepared for some inequality of outcome; for, as every teacher knows, there can be at best equality before the competition, but not after it.

Many are reluctant to admit that all societies are marked by inequalities of their own kind because they fear that such an admission might be construed as a counsel of despair. But that should not be the case. Not all inequalities are of the same kind; they are not all equally odious or intolerable, and they are not all unalterable. Many of the inequalities of the past appear insupportable in the light of our present social and political ideals; such, for example, are the inequalities due to caste and gender, and there is no reason to believe that they cannot be reduced, if not eliminated. But there are other inequalities due, for instance, to education and occupation that cannot be viewed or treated in at all the same way. The two types of inequality are very different in their origins and consequences, and our attitudes towards them should also be different. Making and maintaining clear analytical distinctions between the different types of inequality will help us to avoid tilting at windmills.

Our society is going through many changes. We will miss the significance of these changes if we take the simple view that there were inequalities in the past and there are inequalities in the present, and hence nothing has changed. If we are to address inequality as a question of policy, we have to take a practical view of the problem. A practical view is the opposite of the utopian one which holds that any kind of change is possible; it is also the opposite of the fatalist view which holds that no change is possible. Fatalists and utopians are both contradicted by historical experience which shows that changes have indeed taken place but that those changes have not led to the elimination of all inequalities, whether in India or anywhere else.

* * *

The changes we are now experiencing are no doubt distinctive of our own social and historical conditions. But they are not altogether unique or without historical precedent. There is something to be learnt about what is happening in our society now by comparing our present experience with the experiences of other societies in similar circumstances in the present or the past.

When I look at the changes now taking place in Indian society, I am struck by significant parallels with changes that began in Western societies towards the end of the eighteenth century. Those changes have been examined from a variety of points of view. Here I will consider briefly the account of the political philosopher Alexis de Tocqueville who wrote in the first half of the nineteenth century. Tocqueville was a French aristocrat whose sojourn in the United States convinced him that the old type of society based on hierarchy was being replaced everywhere, at least in the West, by a new type based on equality, and that the change from hierarchy to equality was irreversible. Tocqueville was right on many important points but wrong on some others, and there is as much to learn from his mistakes as from his insights.

Tocqueville contrasted what he called the aristocratic societies of the past with the democratic societies of the present and the future. For him, democracy stood not just for a new type of political system but for a whole new social order with its distinctive laws, customs, manners, and ways of life and thought. Aristocratic society was a society of estates which, like the castes in our traditional order, were ranked by both law and custom, whereas democratic society is a society of citizens and associations of citizens enjoying equality of legal status.

The guiding principle in the movement from aristocratic to democratic societies is the principle of equality. Tocqueville wrote: 'The gradual development of the principle of equality is, therefore, a providential fact. It has all the chief characteristics of such a fact: it is universal, it is lasting, it constantly eludes all human interference, and all events as well as all men contribute to its progress' (Tocqueville 1957, vol. 1, p. 6). He set out to demonstrate the advance of equality in every sphere: in the material conditions of life, in patterns of social interaction, and in ideas, beliefs, and values.

We can now say with the advantage of hindsight that there was a serious flaw in Tocqueville's perception of what was happening around him. For while there was definitely an advance of equality in law, custom, and manners, this advance was accompanied by an increase, and not a decrease, of inequality in the distribution of income. The point I wish to make is a simple one, that the advance of equality, where it does take place, follows a highly uneven course. Through much of the nineteenth century, in most Western countries, economic inequality was increasing in the face of a clear and definite advance of legal equality. I am not suggesting that the same process has to be repeated in India. But we should not be too greatly surprised to find that new forms of inequality are emerging even while old ones are in retreat.

Throughout the nineteenth century in Europe, the old economic and social order was being replaced by a new one. The old order was based on the hierarchy of birth whereas the new one was based on competition and individual mobility. Neither the competition nor the individual mobility operated fairly, freely, or without impediment, but the governing principle of the new order was different from that of the old one. The new principle was summed up in Napoleon's slogan of 'careers open to talent'. For all his sins, Napoleon was a strong advocate of the ideal of equality of opportunity.

Central to the new economic and social order was the emergence of a new occupational system and an educational system corresponding to it. Again, Napoleon played a crucial part in these developments, directly in France and indirectly elsewhere. These developments have now acquired a worldwide significance. We cannot analyse the changing patterns of inequality in contemporary India without taking into account the new occupational and educational systems. Apart from their great economic and social significance, what I would like to stress is their relative novelty. Education and occupation provide a different basis for social identity from what was provided by caste and gender in the past.

Modern occupations are both highly differentiated and elaborately ranked: this is true of modern occupations everywhere, in India and Pakistan no less than in the United States or Russia. The list of individual occupations in any modern economic system runs into thousands or even tens of thousands. The ranking of these individual occupations has been examined by sociologists the world over. While there are variations from one society to another in the details of occupational ranking, there are also many common features. Again, while some individual mobility, both within and between generations, takes place everywhere, its range and frequency vary greatly from one society to another. Individual mobility between lower and higher occupations does not negate occupational stratification, but in fact confirms it.

Modern societies have not done away with inequality, and it is doubtful that they will or can do so in the future. But the inequalities characteristic of them are different from those that prevailed in the past. They are based on a different social principle and their social consequences are different. Modern societies are characterized by what I would call competitive inequality as against the hierarchical inequality characteristic of the past, whether in Europe or in India. We must keep in mind as clearly as possible the distinction between the two principles of inequality if we are to make a proper assessment of the changes now taking place in India.

My aim is not to glorify competitive inequality, but only to point out that it is different from the hierarchical inequality that pervades societies based on estate or caste. Competitive inequality has many ugly faces which become all too visible in a society undergoing a major transformation. John Rawls has spoken against a 'callous meritocratic society' (Rawls 1972), and I find little attraction in the view that the race is to the swiftest and the devil may take the hindmost. At the same time, something can be done to regulate competitive inequality through intelligent and humane social policy. But we will make very little headway if we maintain the posture that competitive inequality can be wished out of existence by an act of collective goodwill.

* * *

Before I end, I would like to return very briefly to the point at which I began. I began by indicating the importance of disciplined social analysis in understanding a complex and changing social reality marked by deep and pervasive contradictions. In order to make that understanding clear and reliable, we have to step back a little from the flow of everyday events. Stepping back enables us to take a broad view of the social reality and to examine it in a comparative and historical perspective. An institution of higher learning does well by itself and by society when it encourages the adoption of a broad historical and comparative view of the social reality.

When I say that an institution should enable those who come to it for their education to step back a little, I do not mean that it is a good thing to remain permanently insulated from the flow of everyday life. Such insulation is neither possible nor desirable. Having pointed to the emergence of a new economic and social order, I cannot turn my back on the need for practical action within it. But practical action is likely to be more and not less fruitful where it is informed by a broad understanding of the laws that govern the movements of society. That understanding does not come automatically from immersion in the flow of everyday events; it can be acquired only through a particular kind of intellectual discipline.

A common response to the many problems by which everyday life is beset is to take recourse to the construction of utopias. The utopian outlook is not an aid but an obstacle to the disciplined analysis of social structure, social conflict, and social change. My aim in discussing the contradictions of equality was to give a sample of the sociological approach, and to show how it differs from the utopian. The utopian approach constructs a world which is free from inequality, contradiction, and conflict. Such a world does not correspond to the social reality anywhere, in either the past or the present. We can cope with inequality, contradiction, and conflict only by analysing their nature and forms, and not by wishing them out of existence.

Utopianism is the enemy not only of social theory but also of social policy. Social policy has very little to offer to those radical egalitarians whose aim is to eradicate every form of inequality, and all at once. It cannot be fruitful or effective if it trains its guns without discrimination on both hierarchical and competitive inequality. Much of the former, such as the practice of untouchability or the exclusion of women from the public domain, can and should be eliminated. We have in the last 50 years achieved some success in these respects, but a great deal more remains to be done.

Inequalities due to income, education, and occupation cannot be eliminated, but they can be regulated. Regulating the inequalities of income may be difficult, but it is not beyond the reach of policy. Similarly, a great deal can be done to expand educational opportunities, although it will be difficult to provide education of the same quality to all members of society and impossible to ensure that they all achieve equal success in their educational careers. Again, while no social policy can eliminate the social ranking of occupations, it should be possible to provide a minimum of security and dignity to all positions, including the lowliest, within the occupational system. But my field of specialization is social theory and not social policy, and therefore I must bring my observations to an end at this point.

References

Aron, Raymond. 1968. *Progress and Disillusion*. London: Pall Mall Press.

Nehru, Jawaharlal. 1961. *The Discovery of India*. Bombay: Asia Publishing House.

Rawls, John. 1972. *A Theory of Justice*. London: Oxford University Press.

Tocqueville, Alexis de. 1957. *Democracy in America*. New York: Alfred Knopf.

Chapter 11

Universities in the Twenty-first Century*

As an institution, the university has a longer span of life than the lifespan of any of its individual members. It was there before most of its present members entered it, and will continue to be there after they leave it. This appearance of continuity masks the many changes taking place both in the internal structure of the university and in its relationship with its environment.

My focus here will be on the changes taking place in the university both as a centre of learning and as a social institution. I believe that we can understand what these changes portend for the future only if we take a longer-term view of them than is usually done in such discussions. I will not discuss any one university in particular but universities in general, and I will not confine myself only to universities in India but also refer from time to time to universities in other parts of the world which have influenced our own universities in the past and will probably continue to influence them even more in the future.

When I entered the service of the University of Delhi in 1959, there were far fewer universities in the country than there are now. They were smaller in size and there was less variety among them. There was of course the distinction between the Central and the state universities, but that did not seem to be such an important difference

*This text is being published in the *Journal of Educational Planning and Administration*, vol. XXIII, no. 4, October 2009, pp. 331–46.

then. So far as I can recall, the category of 'deemed university' or 'deemed to be university' did not exist at that time. When I came from the University of Calcutta, where I had been a student, to become a lecturer in the University of Delhi, I was often reminded of what I had heard about the University of Calcutta as it was 20 or 30 years earlier. I had a certain idea or image of the university as a centre of science and scholarship. Not all the 300 or so university institutions listed today by the Association of Indian Universities correspond very closely to that conception of the university, and I believe that the reality will diverge more and more from it as we move further into the twenty-first century.

Until the beginning of the twentieth century, the universities were not only few in number, they were also small in size. Where the university comprised only a few thousand persons, it could, and in some cases did, function as a community of scientists and scholars among whom there was close and fruitful interaction across the disciplines from physics to philosophy, and between senior and junior members such as professors, lecturers, research scholars, and graduate and undergraduate students. Such close and fruitful interaction did not take place always or everywhere, but it could at least be visualized as a realizable objective.

The universities grew in size throughout the twentieth century but this growth was much more dramatic in some countries than in others. The larger universities in India, such as the universities of Calcutta, Bombay, and Delhi, number their students in hundreds of thousands. It is very difficult for the different parts of such a large organization to remain connected with each other effectively and meaningfully, and to act with a sense of common purpose. When an institution undergoes a large change of scale, its mode of functioning changes and its initial objective becomes displaced.

The change in scale of our universities has come about as a result of pressures of various kinds. The two that I will consider in some detail are the pressure from the growth and expansion of specialized knowledge, and the pressure on the universities to become socially more inclusive. The number of disciplines that a university has to accommodate today is far larger than it was a hundred years ago; and the number of students and, correspondingly of academic and non-academic staff, has also increased enormously. These are the two issues with which I will deal sequentially, but before that I would like to set down the ideals of the modern university as they came to be established in the course of the nineteenth century.

* * *

The nineteenth century witnessed the emergence and growth of the modern university, beginning with the establishment of the University of Berlin in 1810. There were no doubt universities before that time—at Bologna, Paris, Oxford, Cairo, and elsewhere—but they were very different from the modern universities that came to be established gradually in the nineteenth century and to flourish in the twentieth. We have only to look back from the beginning of the twentieth century to the beginning of the nineteenth to appreciate the significance of the changes that came about in the course of a hundred years. At the beginning of the nineteenth century, Harvard, Yale, and Princeton were universities only in name; they were basically colleges for undergraduate education, and very different from the great centres of science and scholarship that they became in the course of the twentieth century. Oxford and Cambridge had gone into a long period of hibernation from which they gradually shook themselves up in the course of the nineteenth century. The universities had sunk to such low levels in France that Napoleon turned his attention away from them to the newly established *grandes écoles* or great schools for producing a new breed of administrators, engineers, and teachers to serve the nation.

As it happened, a new beginning in the life of the university was just then being made in Germany. Germany was by no means the most advanced country in Europe economically or culturally, but it had better universities at Jena, Heidelberg, Göttingen, and elsewhere than its more advanced Western neighbours. The architect of the new university was the philologist and philosopher Wilhelm von Humboldt, then minister for education in Prussia. The university he helped to establish in Berlin in 1810 became a model for universities in many parts of the world. It was named at first after the Prussian ruler, but later renamed after its real founder as the Humboldt University of Berlin. Its creation helped to revive the universities and provided a new institutional framework for the organization of science and scholarship in many countries.

Not many believed at that time that the universities were worth reviving. 'In France, neither Tocqueville nor Constant thought seriously about the universities, and they had no great expectations that they would contribute much to the effective operation of free institutions. In Scotland, Adam Smith had a rather low opinion of universities and university teachers, although he was a university teacher for a good part of his life. He certainly did not regard universities as the intellectual engines of liberal society. John Stuart Mill did not expect any great help for liberalism or democracy from universities' (Shils 1997: 252).

Humboldt's ideas for the regeneration of the university met with opposition in his own country. 'He was also writing against a strong current of opinion in Germany which favoured the abolition of universities and their replacement for teaching and training purposes by specialized professional schools—as Napoleon had done in France—and by concentrating research in academies or learned societies' (ibid.: 235). Those who value the modern university as a centre of advanced study and research should be thankful that Humboldt held his ground and had his way.

The new type of university, first set up in Berlin, is referred to by some as the Humboldtian university. New universities were set up and existing ones reorganized under its influence. The first university of the new type to be set up in the United States was the Johns Hopkins University established in 1876. Thereafter Stanford University was set up in 1885 and the University of Chicago in 1891. Harvard, Yale, Princeton, and other institutions were reorganized under its influence. Its influence reached India later, and that too in a vague and attenuated form.

* * *

The new type of university retained the aspiration of the old one to accommodate all the principal branches of study within its scope. When the first universities were set up in India in the nineteenth century, that was the implicit understanding, although they themselves did not undertake much research or even teaching in their early phase of existence. New branches of science and scholarship began to emerge throughout the nineteenth century, and this tendency became accentuated in the twentieth. In the twenty-first century, it has become increasingly difficult for a university to cover every branch of knowledge and yet retain its coherence and unity as an institution unless the conditions are exceptionally favourable. As a consequence, either the universities are bursting at the seams, as at Calcutta, Bombay, and Delhi, or new universities with a more limited scope and a sharper focus are coming up, as for example, agricultural universities, universities of juridical sciences, and, of course, the National University of Educational Planning and Administration.

The new type of university which followed the model of Humboldt adopted three fundamental principles. These may be described as (i) the unity of teaching and research, (ii) the freedom to teach and to learn, and (iii) the principle of self-governance. These three principles served to inspire modern universities in many parts of the world, including India. They were the ideals of the university in the nineteenth and twentieth centuries, although the ideals were not fully realized in any university, including the University of Berlin.

Wilhelm von Humboldt set great store by the unity of teaching and research. He was himself an outstanding scholar of the humanities, and his younger brother, Alexander von Humboldt, an outstanding naturalist. They both participated directly and actively in exploring new fields of science and scholarship.

Until Humboldt's time, research was done only occasionally and sporadically in the universities and colleges. They were engaged principally in the transmission and, at best, the criticism of existing knowledge, rather than the creation of new knowledge. The advance of knowledge had in the past been slow and uneven. Things began to change from the end of the eighteenth century when knowledge began to advance on many fronts. Humboldt, unlike Napoleon, felt that the university should be in the forefront of this advance. There was nothing inevitable about his move, but it had momentous consequences for the development of science and scholarship.

In a world in which knowledge accumulates slowly and intellectual horizons are constrained by geographical boundaries, the college or university teacher may not be expected to do much more than to master the existing body of knowledge in his field and to transmit a part of it to his students. This is still what we expect from the conscientious teacher in a good secondary school, and probably not much more was expected from teachers in most colleges and universities before the nineteenth century.

In the course of the twentieth century, some of the leading universities such as Harvard, Yale, Princeton, Stanford, and Chicago came to be known as 'research universities'. Their growth was accompanied by the growth of the 'mass universities'. This distinction is acknowledged in the United States and possibly also in China, but not in India. Edward Shils (1997: 14) has described the mass university 'as a university with more than twenty thousand students' and has observed, 'The mass university has brought into the university many young persons whose foremost and perhaps exclusive aim is to obtain a degree and to enter a remunerative occupation' (ibid.: 45). Although he was speaking of universities in the United States, his remarks apply with particular force to the situation in India. Shils, it may be pointed out, was a member of the Indian Education Commission of 1964–6, known widely as the Kothari Commission.

Having become established by the end of the nineteenth century, the research universities acquired their own momentum in the United States, and moved in directions that could hardly have been foreseen by Humboldt in 1810. As the results of research came to be widely disseminated, distinction in research began to attract public attention as against success in teaching. Particularly after World War II, the pressure to be productive in research began to be increasingly felt in the better universities.

The research universities began to compete with each other in terms of the quality and quantity of the output of their professors. Rating agencies undertook to rank the different universities according to their general standing and according to their standing in particular disciplines. Presidents and deans undertook to attract stars to their universities with offers of generous terms and conditions. The talent search was not confined to universities in the United States but was extended to countries throughout the world, including India. This kind of open and undisguised competition to attract scientists and scholars of national and even international renown undermined the unity of teaching and research because today a star is a star by virtue of his research and not his teaching.

The freedom to teach and to learn is recognized as an essential feature in the operation of the modern university. Where the university is expected to explore and examine new fields of knowledge instead of merely transmitting the conventional wisdom, the freedom to teach and to learn becomes indispensable. The creation of new knowledge cannot be fruitfully undertaken without the continuous criticism of existing knowledge. The active encouragement of critical enquiry has come to be viewed as integral to the institutions of science and scholarship.

In many countries the exercise of academic freedom is now taken for granted in the universities. This was not always the case in the past, and it is not the case in all countries even today. The exercise of academic freedom was a relatively new phenomenon in the early part of the nineteenth century. Most of the older universities such as those at Paris, Oxford, and Cambridge were in some sense handmaidens of the church, which often maintained close scrutiny over what was said or written in them. This was true of medieval centres of learning in most parts of the world. The universities took time to free themselves from religious control whereas such freedom could be more easily exercised in the learned societies and associations that began to emerge outside the universities in the wake of the European Enlightenment.

The principle of academic freedom or the freedom of enquiry in science and scholarship gathered strength in the universities throughout the nineteenth century. Once the dam of religious opposition to free enquiry was breached, the universities transformed themselves as both centres of learning and social institutions. By the middle of the twentieth century, the universities in the West had effectively become secular institutions. We have in that respect had the advantage that our first universities at Calcutta, Bombay, and Madras were secular institutions and free from regulation by religious authorities from their very inception. Religious education was excluded from the university's curriculum: at Calcutta, 'the Senate reiterated the principle that no question should be asked in the examination that required an expression of religious belief on the part of the candidate' (Chattopadhyay 2007: 21).

Academic freedom may be compromised even in a secular environment, for the threat to it can come not only from the church but also from the state. In the last century, the freedom to teach and the freedom to learn were severely restricted by the Soviet state. Under Stalin, the universities were not handmaidens of the church; they became handmaidens of the party. Whether in teaching or in research, the universities had to stay within the limits prescribed by the state and its watchdogs in a whole range of disciplines from plant genetics to the philosophy of language.

In democratic countries such as Britain, France, and India, the state does not interfere openly or directly with teaching and research in the universities. But to the extent that it controls the purse strings on which the flow of funds depends, it does influence priorities in teaching and research indirectly and in the long run.

Restraints on the freedom to teach in the classroom or to publish in accordance with one's considered judgement may be created by popular pressure or the anticipation of a public outcry. One cannot today express oneself freely and frankly about the lives and deeds of such iconic figures as Chhatrapati Shivaji, Netaji Subhash Chandra Bose, or Dr B.R. Ambedkar. A lecture or publication which seeks to do so may cause an outcry and even lead to a violent protest. Similar consequences may follow if offence is caused, albeit inadvertently, to the sentiments of a religious minority or a backward community. This kind of situation is most likely to prevail in the mass universities which have become ascendant since the middle of the twentieth century.

By and large, in the course of the nineteenth century, the universities promoted a spirit of critical enquiry about man and the natural and social world that he inhabited, and carried that spirit forward into the twentieth century and beyond. They also provided increasing room for political debate and discussion. With the great expansion of universities after World War II and, in particular, with the emergence of the mass universities, they became leading centres of political dissent. Increasingly, they came to enjoy a kind of freedom that opposition parties did not always have. While critical enquiry in science and scholarship and political dissent may be related to each other, they are not one and the same thing. Pervasive political dissent, unrelated or remotely related to the ends of science and scholarship, has increasingly led to severe dislocation in the regularity and routine of academic work. Where the institutions of science and scholarship are weak, this kind of dislocation becomes endemic.

The freedom to express dissenting views has led students in the larger metropolitan universities, sometimes with the encouragement of their teachers, to espouse radical political causes. Strikes, rallies, and demonstrations are regularly organized, and an antinomian and emancipationist atmosphere is created. It may well be the case that only a small and determined minority of persons, among both students and teachers, seriously espouse these causes, but they are allowed to prevail because of the indifference and apathy of the majority who simply stay away. This is a far cry from the nineteenth-century ideal of the university as a community of scholars and scientists who would be free to study and teach and publish the fruits of their research without fear or favour.

The university was designed to be a community of scholars and scientists responsible for the regulation of their own affairs. The principle of self-governance goes back to the tradition of the medieval corporation in Europe whose right to regulate its own affairs was generally confirmed by the grant of charters. In medieval Europe the universities were among the early examples of corporations in the legal sense of the term, and it is commonly believed that Harvard University was the first corporation in that sense in the United States. Self-governance was accompanied in the case of the universities by a degree of seclusion from the outside world.

In India, the first modern universities were established, not so much by communities of scholars and scientists as by the government of the day. It is no accident that the first three universities were set up in the three presidency capitals of Calcutta, Bombay, and Madras by the colonial government just before the country came formally under the British crown. Just as Oxford and Cambridge still carry the vestiges of their monastic past, our universities bear many of the marks of their origin in colonial rule.

The colonial civil servants who took responsibility for the establishment of our universities included many who had had experience of the best universities in England. Sir Henry Maine, who was one of the early vice-chancellors of the University of Calcutta, had been a professor at Cambridge. No doubt the colonial rulers of India meant well by the universities they were setting up, but it is not clear to what extent they believed that self-government was a realizable objective in India; rightly or wrongly, they never tired of pointing out the absence of such a tradition in the country that they had brought under their rule.

Such self-governance as the universities were allowed was exercised under the watchful eyes of the government. The early vice-chancellors of the Indian universities were British, although they were replaced by Indian vice-chancellors before very long. The heads of Indian universities acquired the habit of accommodation to the existing powers in the early decades of their existence, an accommodation that became strengthened rather than weakened after the transfer of power. It was only the exceptional vice-chancellor, such as Sir Ashutosh Mukherji in the University of Calcutta before independence, or Dr M.S. Gore at the University of Bombay after it, who stood his ground against the government.

In recent decades, the great expansion in the size of the university and in its scale of operation has made academic self-government increasingly difficult. The administrative component of many universities has become as important as their academic component, and in some respects more important. In the larger universities, the administrative staff number in their thousands. They tend to spend more time in the university and to know more about its daily operation than the professors. The academic and the administrative staff have both become unionized, and when the unions act in concert, they might count for more than the constituted authorities of the universities such as the academic council, the board of research studies, and the faculty.

The bureaucratization of the universities is not an altogether new phenomenon. Writing nearly a hundred years ago, Max Weber (1948) had noted its beginnings in the German universities, at that time the objects of admiration among academics in many parts of the world. Closer to our times, Edward Shils noted,

> As a result the administrative staffs proliferate and academics find themselves surrounded on all sides by administrators, who want forms filled out, who wish to have their permission sought to do things for which older academics do not recall having had to seek permission. Rules, forms and 'channels' become more prominent; informal understandings and conventions become less prominent in the administration of universities (1997: 34).

Shils was writing with the American university mainly in mind; the problem is of course much more acute in India.

The authorities of the universities have now not only larger numbers of students and teachers to take care of, they have to secure and manage increasingly larger budgets. They have to supplement the traditional administrative skills with those of effective and successful fund management. It is said that the wealthier private universities in the United States are becoming organized like business firms. Enthusiasts for private universities in India are perhaps not all aware of the problems that are now being faced by some of the most renowned universities in the United States such as Chicago, Princeton, and Stanford (Shapiro 1992).

* * *

The traditional idea of the university was that it would provide a home, within the confines of a single institution, for the cultivation of all significant branches of knowledge. It was this idea that Humboldt sought to carry forward at the most advanced levels of teaching and research when he established the University of Berlin in 1810. The institutions that Napoleon was promoting in France at about the same time were different in both principle and practice from the university in its medieval or its reconstituted form. The *grandes écoles* emerged as great institutions, but they did not seek to accommodate every significant branch of knowledge in any one single institution.

In an important work on the American university, Talcott Parsons and Gerald Platt gave expression to a view of the university that was still close to the model of Humboldt that had been carried over from Berlin to Harvard in the course of the nineteenth century. They wrote, 'Concern with knowledge and its advancement is analytically independent of its practical uses' (Parsons and Platt 1973: 33), emphasizing that the main concern of the university was with the former and not the latter. Napoleon, on the other hand, had the practical uses of knowledge very much in mind when he decided to put his weight behind the *grandes écoles*.

Parsons and Platt believed that the university as an institution for the advancement of knowledge had a distinctive intellectual core. That core, according to them, consisted of the arts and sciences, meaning academic disciplines such as physics, chemistry, mathematics, languages, history, and sociology. They knew of course that subjects such as law, medicine, and engineering had also been accommodated by the American university. These they believed to belong to its periphery rather than its core. The *école polytechnique*, perhaps the most renowned among the *grandes écoles*, was, on the other hand, set up with the specific objective of training engineers for service in the civil and military branches of the government. With the advantage of hindsight, we may view it as a great precursor of our Indian Institutes of Technology (IITs).

If the university is to function as an intellectual community, or a community of scientists and scholars, is it possible for it in the twenty-first century to accommodate all branches of learning, theoretical and practical, and to deal with them even-handedly and meaningfully? The universities of the twenty-first century are very different places from what the University of Berlin was in the 1820s or even what Harvard University was in the 1920s when Parsons began his career there.

Even though Harvard maintains its pre-eminent position as a research university, it has changed a very great deal. With close to 20,000 students, it is no longer either very small or very cohesive. Its various constituent units, such as the faculty of arts and sciences, the faculty of medicine, the law school, the business school, and the school of public health, largely operate separately although they all bear the Harvard label. Some of them have huge budgets whose management and control are exercised to a large extent independently of each other. Whatever may have been the past significance of the faculty of arts and sciences, it no longer overshadows all the other components of the university.

At the symposium on Universities of the Twenty-first Century held at Chicago in 1991, dean Rosovsky of Harvard lamented the decline of academic citizenship in his time. 'When it concerns our more important obligations—academic citizenship—neither rule nor custom is any longer compelling' (Rosovsky 1992: 187). In the mass universities that are growing rapidly today, not only are the obligations of academic citizenship treated lightly, but to many incoming members the very idea of it might appear strange and unfamiliar.

The idea of the university as a community of scientists and scholars of whom many, if not most, feel bound by the obligations of academic citizenship has become remote from the reality, certainly in India, but not in India alone. Yet, the idea of the university as a community continues to have a hold on the minds of many academics, if only as a form of nostalgia. This nostalgia is sustained in part by an oral tradition regarding the exciting and unconstrained intellectual interchanges among scholars and scientists in the senior common rooms of Oxford and Cambridge, which a few of our own more privileged academics had witnessed or experienced in the past. It is doubtful that that kind of intellectual life can be recreated in the twenty-first century even in Oxford and Cambridge, leave alone the universities in India.

The pressure on the universities to accommodate new branches of study has increased enormously in the last few decades. The expansion of knowledge has been accompanied by differentiation between and within academic disciplines. The universities themselves played no small part in the expansion and the differentiation. The universities have today found accommodation for many new subjects that had hardly any existence in Humboldt's time or even a hundred years later. The proliferation of disciplines now threatens the viability of the university as a single institution for advanced study and research in all subjects.

'The growth of knowledge,' it has been said, 'is a disorderly movement' (Shils 1975: 125; see also Parsons and Platt 1973: vi–vii). New ideas come up and fade away; only a few of them bear fruit. The ones that fructify do not remain active for long. It is in the long-term interest of society to encourage new ideas, new methods of enquiry, and new areas of investigation to grow even when they appear unpromising to begin with. But is it necessary or desirable to turn every new field of study into an academic discipline in order to find a place for it in the university? Today, at least in India, but not only in India, universities seem to be in competition with each other to attract and accommodate every new field of study. It is now becoming a common practice in our universities to attract and accommodate what are called 'self-financing courses' in order to augment their revenues. Promoters of these self-financing courses have often shown great ingenuity in devising new subjects for inclusion in the university curriculum.

Until the beginning of the twentieth century, the universities were not very eager to accommodate new or emerging branches of study. Disciplines such as anthropology, demography, psychology, sociology, and statistics first grew outside the universities before they found places within them. It is not that new disciplines were kept out of the universities for ever, but the universities took their time to allow them in. In the nineteenth century, the learned societies and associations took a more active part in the growth of new fields of enquiry.

All through the nineteenth century the balance among disciplines underwent change in the universities. This change was in part the outcome of the growth of secular science and scholarship. The older European universities, at Paris, Oxford, and Cambridge, gave pride of place to theology, philosophy, and classical languages and literature. Those subjects are still taught, but even in the older universities they have now lost their pride of place. Theology is not taught in many of the newer universities which might instead provide for teaching and research in comparative religion, or the history or sociology of religion.

In the English-speaking universities the social sciences grew out of moral philosophy, and the natural sciences out of natural philosophy. There was some continuity but there was also a great deal of change. Issues relating to society, economy, and polity were no doubt discussed and debated in the older universities, but they became subjects of systematic enquiry only in the nineteenth century. Systematic empirical investigations into social life were first undertaken outside the universities, by such persons as Frédéric Le Play in France and Charles Booth in England. It was only in the twentieth century that such studies became incorporated into programmes of teaching and research in the universities. Survey research has now become an integral part of the social sciences. Today it is undertaken both within and outside the universities, and it is not easy to argue that the universities enjoy any unique advantage in conducting such studies.

The transformation of 'natural philosophy' into the natural sciences began a little earlier, but here again many of the initial steps, particularly in England and France, were taken outside the universities. In the eighteenth century, both Henry Cavendish in England and Antoine-Laurent Lavoisier in France conducted their pioneering studies outside the universities. This was largely true even of Charles Darwin in the nineteenth century.

By the beginning of the twentieth century, the universities had reclaimed the major branches of science and scholarship. That century, and particularly its first half, witnessed the highest ascendancy of the universities as centres of science and scholarship. Between the two World Wars, for someone with a vocation for science and scholarship almost anywhere in the world, a university would be the place of first choice. It provided a modest but secure livelihood, a relatively tranquil atmosphere for study and reflection, well-endowed libraries and laboratories, the companionship of colleagues and students, and the occasional excitement of working at or even beyond the frontiers of existing knowledge. There were not many such places outside the universities then.

As I have indicated, a new balance of disciplines began to take shape in the universities from the middle of the nineteenth century onwards. It became gradually established in Europe and America, and then extended its influence over the new universities that were coming into being all over the world. It appeared in many variations, but by the middle of the twentieth century, the new balance, with the arts and sciences at the core and the professional subjects at the periphery, had acquired a certain stability. There is no reason to expect that this balance will remain unchanged for the rest of time. University institutions have grown and diversified to such an extent throughout the world since the middle of the twentieth century that it may be unrealistic to expect that any single model—whether the 'Oxbridge' or the 'Harvard' model—will be the predominant model everywhere.

New universities are coming up at a rapid rate in countries with very diverse intellectual traditions and socio-political orientations. The Chinese have built a very large number of new universities in the last two or three decades with objectives that are different from those with which universities were established in the nineteenth century or even in the first half of the twentieth century, and it is unlikely that their intellectual foundations will be the same as those of the earlier universities.

The emphasis in many countries that are now creating new universities is on engineering and management, conceived in a broad way rather than on the arts and sciences in the traditional sense. China, which had only a few universities until 1976, is now producing more PhDs in engineering than the United States (Li et al. 2008). Perhaps the new type of university that will acquire ascendancy there will have science, technology, and management at its core and the humanities and social sciences at the periphery. Such a model will have a natural appeal for those who believe that the main purpose of tertiary education is to produce the trained manpower needed for rapid economic growth.

* * *

Today the creation and expansion of universities is driven not only by pressures to accommodate new subjects, or new branches or variants of existing subjects. It is driven also by the pressure on the universities to become socially more inclusive by accommodating students as well as teachers from all classes and communities, and women as well as men.

When the universities were given a new lease of life, starting with the creation of the University of Berlin, it was not the intention of the reformers and innovators to make university education available to all members of society. Even school education was far from being within everyone's reach. The nineteenth-century university was an 'aristocratic' rather than a 'popular' institution, if not always in principle, at least generally in practice. Here Napoleon was clearly in advance of Humboldt. It was the *grandes écoles* that instituted the practice of recruiting students through open national competition or the *concours général.* However, those institutions were, and have remained, elitist in their own way. They replaced an aristocracy of birth by a meritocracy of talent; and of course they remained closed to women throughout the nineteenth century.

All through the nineteenth century and into the twentieth, restrictions on entry into universities on social grounds, that is, on grounds of religion, race, caste, or gender came to be eased. By the middle of the twentieth century such restrictions had lost much of their force in most countries. This of course does not mean that all castes and communities, or that even both women and men are to be found in all universities in proportion to their strength in the population. Even though women have not achieved complete parity with men, they have in most countries fared better than disadvantaged castes and communities.

The reasons for this difference are fascinating, but I am unable to enter into a discussion of those reasons on the present occasion.

In the nineteenth century, university education was for only a few and not the majority or even a numerically significant minority of the population. So long as the universities were few in number and small in size, only a few members of society could realistically form expectations of entering a university even where no formal restrictions on their entry existed. Education in a university was viewed as a privilege rather than a right. Today it is increasingly regarded as a right, at least by many of those who meet the minimum requirements of eligibility for admission, and the requirements themselves tend to be relaxed under political pressure.

Social and economic changes in the nineteenth and early part of the twentieth century led to changes in the expectations of people. More and more of them became aware of the entitlements of citizenship. As elementary education became universal and secondary education more extensive and widespread, increasing numbers of persons turned their thoughts to tertiary education. For members of the growing middle class, a college or university degree appeared indispensable both for its practical utility and its symbolic value. The demand for a university education, or at least a university degree, grew with the growth of the middle class.

The conclusion of World War II and the termination of colonial rule dramatically altered the prospects for tertiary education throughout the world. The proximate causes for the expansion of tertiary education differed from one country to another, but the outcome was similar everywhere. The universities opened their doors, if not to everyone, then to increasing numbers of persons. Just as the middle of the nineteenth century ushered in the secularization of the universities, so the middle of the twentieth century saw their democratization.

In the United States, the end of World War II created unprecedented opportunities for returning soldiers to enter a university and receive a university degree. The Servicemen's Readjustment Act of 1944, popularly known as the GI Bill of Rights, was designed to serve more than one objective. It was designed as a token of gratitude to those who had risked death and endured hardship in the service of the nation. It was designed also to meet the need for qualified manpower, particularly graduates in the sciences in the post-war economy. Until its enactment, university funding in the United States had come mainly from private sources or from the states. After it, the federal government became increasingly involved in university funding, and expansion of the tertiary sector in education became more consciously linked with manpower planning.

The colonial government, which set up the first universities in modern India, did so with limited aims and objectives. It did not expect the universities to bring about either a revolution in learning or a social revolution. The funding it provided was on a modest scale and it had to be supplemented by private philanthropy. The universities did contribute to the making of a new middle class with new attitudes and aspirations, but their influence did not spread very far or go very deep.

This began to change with the coming of independence. The makers of modern India had benefited from university education, whether in India or abroad, and wanted its benefits to be made widely available. Almost immediately after being set up, the first government of independent India constituted a University Education Commission under Dr S. Radhakrishnan who had served as a professor at both Calcutta and Oxford. Its attitude towards the universities was different from that of the colonial government. It expected more from them and it was prepared to fund them more generously. Soon bonds became established between a well-disposed and munificent government and those in the universities who were hungry for their expansion. They acquired the habit of turning to the government for meeting their every need. The government has encouraged the hunger for expansion that has grown in the universities, but it has satisfied that hunger only to some extent and on its own terms. Governments rarely view the pursuit of science and scholarship as an end in itself, but mainly as a means to other ends.

In independent India the programme for building universities became consciously aligned with the needs of development and democracy. The objectives of the university had changed between Humboldt's time and the middle of the twentieth century; or, rather, the university had acquired new objectives without fully renouncing the old ones. This was inevitable in view of the fact that different universities in the different parts of the world had to adapt themselves to different kinds of social and political environment.

In the newly independent countries, determined to catch up economically and educationally with the advanced countries, the idea of the university as an 'ivory tower', detached from the practical concerns of the outside world, did not have much appeal. Prominent scientists and scholars came forward to show what the universities could do to eliminate poverty, reduce inequality, and establish a scientific temper. Far from wanting to insulate the universities from the outside world, they wanted them to reach forward to it and to make their contribution to economic development and social change.

Today in India, the universities are expected to contribute directly to the pursuit and promotion of equality. This is perhaps natural in a country which at the time of independence had inherited a remarkably hierarchical social system. The relationship between a country's system of higher education and its system of inequality is a complex one which is often misunderstood and misrepresented. The universities have contributed something to individual mobility and can contribute more. But they have also contributed to the reproduction of inequality, and this often appears to offset their contribution to individual mobility.

More than 60 years after independence, India is still not an inclusive society in any meaningful sense. Hundreds of millions of persons not only have no access to a university, they do not even know what it means to have a university education. The pressures on the universities to become socially more inclusive and to contribute, directly and indirectly, to the making of an inclusive society have grown stronger. There are no shortcuts to that end, but the temptation to turn to universities for providing such shortcuts has increased steadily. Where their adoption threatens the academic integrity of the university, vice-chancellors, deans, and professors look the other way.

In a society where deep and pervasive inequalities continue to exist, the universities find it far more difficult to admit and appoint persons from all occupational strata—the offspring of agricultural labourers and stone breakers as well as of judges and businessmen—than to provide representation to all castes and communities in proportion to their strength in the population. Managing quotas based on caste and community has become a major preoccupation of the universities today. In 2006–7, the central universities were required to increase the numbers of their students and teachers suddenly and dramatically in order to make up for shortfalls in the quotas set for them.

In order to meet their quotas, the universities have not only had to increase the numbers of students and teachers, they have also had to relax their standards for admissions and appointments. The relaxation of academic standards in response to social and political pressures has become a standard practice in the universities since independence, and increasingly so in the last couple of decades. It is an open secret which the authorities of the universities do not like to be aired in public. To even hint at the possibility that there might be some contradiction between the demands of social inclusion and the advancement of learning would be to invite the charge of 'elitism', which in India no self-regarding academic would like to bring upon himself.

As the universities have grown in size, the larger ones among them have become more and more disorganized and difficult to manage; and the smaller ones follow the examples set by the larger. For those at the helm of affairs, the problems of administration and management take precedence over academic problems. The regularity and routine of academic life are frequently interrupted; admissions cannot be completed on time; and vacant posts remain unfilled for months and even years. The authorities of the university are frequently locked in combat with unions of students, teachers, and non-academic staff.

The idea of a research university never really acquired roots in the Indian soil. Today, very few persons in any Indian university are seriously engaged in the creation of new knowledge. Even the transmission of existing knowledge is seriously hampered by the poor quality of libraries and laboratories, and the indifference and apathy of all around. Absenteeism among teachers as well as students has become an acknowledged and established feature of many universities in the country. The unions are often so powerful that the authorities of the university have no choice but to condone absenteeism and other forms of dereliction.

At the same time, the number of universities as well as of university students and teachers is increasing. All the indications are that this increase will continue into the foreseeable future. Planners and policymakers are worried that we are not producing enough graduates or enough PhDs, and that other countries are ahead of us. The twenty-first-century university in India will have to meet many different demands. The demands of science and scholarship or of advanced study and research are by no means the only ones with which they have to contend. They have to meet the demand to provide more young men and women with university degrees and diplomas. University graduates are still unevenly distributed among the various castes and communities in Indian society. This disparity is considered unfair and unjust, and the universities are therefore expected to not only produce more graduates but also to ensure that those graduates are more evenly distributed in society.

The declining minority of university teachers who are seriously committed to teaching and research are dismayed by the preoccupation, not to say obsession, with examination and certification in our universities. But the preoccupation is not new. The first universities in modern India were set up in the presidency capitals of Calcutta, Bombay, and Madras not so much to undertake research, or even teaching, as to conduct examinations and confer degrees. Writing on the occasion of the sesquicentennial of the University of Calcutta, Basudeb Chattopadhyay observed, 'Thus the University was set up in 1857 primarily with the task of holding examinations and conferring degrees on successful candidates' (2007: 22), and the same observation may have been made about the two other universities set up in that year. The teaching was done mainly in the colleges, and some research was undertaken by the learned societies and associations such as the Asiatic Society and the Indian Association for the Cultivation of Science. The first, and so far the only, Indian Nobel laureate in science, Sir C.V. Raman entered the services of the University of Calcutta after establishing his credentials as a scientist through his research in the Indian Association for the Cultivation of Science (Venkataraman 1994: 29–42).

One of the first things that had to be determined for the new universities in their early years was their jurisdiction. The territorial jurisdictions of the first three universities were wide to begin with, but they became progressively reduced with the opening of new universities whose jurisdictions were carved out of those of the existing ones. These jurisdictions were essentially jurisdictions for conducting examinations and conferring degrees on students who were taught in various colleges in a widely dispersed geographical area.

Between their beginning in the middle of the nineteenth century and roughly the period of World War I, the Indian universities were too small and their jurisdiction too scattered for them to conduct advanced study and research in a purposeful way. The beginnings of serious study and research were made in a few universities such as Calcutta, Allahabad, and Bombay between the two World Wars. But the promise that many saw in those universities began to fade soon after independence when one after another they became converted into mass universities. Before they could establish a proper programme that would embody the unity of teaching and research, they had to contend with a new kind of institution dedicated to research rather than teaching, such as the laboratories under the Council for Scientific and Industrial Research and the institutes and centres under the Indian Council of Social Science Research.

With the twenty-first century we have entered the era of the mass university. But the nostalgia for a different kind of university in which teaching and research are combined at the most advanced level in all significant branches of knowledge survives in the minds of many who have been exposed to the experience of universities in Europe and America or to legends about the University of Calcutta in the 1920s and 1930s or the University of Delhi in the 1950s and 1960s. We must see that this nostalgia does not become an impediment to the creation of more purposeful though perhaps less ambitious institutions of teaching and research in the twenty-first century.

References

Chattopadhyay, Basudeb. 2007. 'The University of Calcutta: An Overview', *University News*, vol. 45, no. 4 (Special Issue), pp. 15–49.

Li, Yao, John Nalley, Shunming Zhang, and Xiliang Zhao. 2008. 'The Higher Educational Transformation of China and Its Global Implication', Cambridge, Mass., National Bureau of Economic Research, Working Paper.

Parsons, Talcott and Gerald M. Platt. 1973. *The American University*. Cambridge, Massachusetts: Harvard University Press.

Rosovsky, Henry. 1992. 'Comments', *Minerva*, vol. XXXII, no. 2, pp. 183–7.

Shapiro, Harold T. 1992. 'The Functions and Resources of the American University of the Twenty-First Century', *Minerva*, vol. XXXII, no. 2, pp. 163–74.

Shils, Edward. 1975. *Center and Periphery*. Chicago: University of Chicago Press.

———. 1997. *The Calling of Education*. Chicago: University of Chicago Press.

Venkataraman, G. 1994. *Journey Into Light*. New Delhi: Penguin Books.

Weber, Max. 1948. *From Max Weber: Essays in Sociology* (edited by H.H. Gerth and C.W. Mills). New York: Oxford University Press.

Chapter
12

The Viable University*

Are there any basic conditions that have to be met if the university is to be viable as an institution for the pursuit of science and scholarship? This is a difficult and contentious subject on which those who occupy positions of authority and dignity rarely speak on ceremonial occasions such as a university convocation. Since I occupy no such position, I shall take the liberty of addressing this question plainly and candidly.

Universities had been in existence for almost a hundred years when the country became independent in 1947. The first among them were set up under colonial rule to serve a specific set of objectives. In the early decades of their existence, their main objectives were the regulation of syllabuses, the conduct of examinations, and the award of degrees. Teaching was done in the colleges and some research was done in institutions such as the Asiatic Society and the Association for the Cultivation of Science. There were also various Surveys, such as the Geological Survey, the Archaeological Survey, and the Botanical Survey, which undertook research of a certain kind.

Having become established, the universities, or at least some among them, began to aim higher. Some of the Indian vice-chancellors were outstanding personalities who did not share the sceptical attitude of their British counterparts towards the prospects of the Indian

*This is the text of the convocation address delivered at the West Bengal National University of Juridical Sciences on 20 February 2010.

university as a centre of learning. Sir Ashutosh Mukherji initiated the process of building postgraduate departments in the arts and the sciences in the University of Calcutta in the early decades of the twentieth century. These departments sought to embody the unity of teaching and research, and brought together scholars and scientists of the highest rank. The work they did in the university achieved great renown, and they set an example for academics throughout the country.

But it has to be remembered that these centres of excellence in science and scholarship were few and far between and they were small in size. Their material resources were limited, but they were insulated from social and political pressures to provide open access to all. They were selective in their admissions and appointments, and they expanded slowly and in response to the growth of science and scholarship throughout the world.

Outside a few islands of excellence, the production of graduates remained the main preoccupation for those responsible for the support and maintenance of the universities from their inception till the time of independence. From the middle of the nineteenth century onwards, the universities played an important part in the growth and expansion of a new middle class by providing the education and the certification necessary for securing employment as clerks, teachers, doctors, lawyers, administrators, managers, and so on. 'Advancement of Learning' may have been the motto of the University of Calcutta from the start, but those who knocked at its portals in increasing numbers did so less from the thirst for disinterested knowledge than from the prospects for middle-class employment opened up by a university degree. The new middle class needed the universities because without them, entry into that class and advancement within it would be impossible.

* * *

Many of those who genuinely hoped for the advancement of learning felt that the independence of India would provide a new departure in the life of the university which could be made into a real home for science and scholarship. There were good reasons behind the hope for a new beginning. The colonial administration was at best half-hearted in its support for the universities it had created and maintained. It did not support them for being repositories of the values for which the universities stood in Europe and America, but for the more limited purpose of producing the manpower necessary for running the imperial system.

At first, things seemed to augur well for a new beginning for the universities in independent India. Jawaharlal Nehru, the first prime minister, placed a high value on science and scholarship, and took a personal interest in their advancement. He himself had never studied in an Indian university, but his experience of Cambridge, one of the great universities of the world, had given him a sense of the part the university could play in the life of a nation.

In a convocation address to the University of Allahabad in the very first year of independence, Nehru had emphasized the values which the universities, as centres of science and scholarship, embodied. He had said, 'A university stands for humanism, for tolerance, for progress, for the adventure of ideas and for the search for truth. It stands for the onward march of the human race towards ever higher objectives. If the universities discharge their duties adequately, then it is well with the nation and the people.' He also struck a note of warning, for he went on to say, 'But if the temple of learning itself becomes a home of narrow bigotry and petty objectives, how then will the nation prosper or a people grow in stature?' (Nehru 1958: 333).

Nehru obviously had forebodings about the disruptive role that factionalism and the divisions of caste and community could play in the universities, and he did not hesitate to speak his mind on the subject. At a convocation of the Aligarh Muslim University held barely a month after the Allahabad convocation, he said, 'I do not like this university being called the Muslim University just as I do not like the Benares University to be called the Hindu University' (ibid.: 338). Which leader of this great nation can speak like that today?

Despite their forebodings, Nehru and his colleagues sought to move forward with the creation of more and better institutions for the nurturance of science and scholarship. The new government wasted no time in setting up a University Education Commission under Dr S. Radhakrishnan in 1948. Radhakrishnan had been a professor of philosophy at the University of Calcutta in its best years, and later became the Spalding Professor at Oxford. Like Nehru, he wanted the university to be an open and secular institution and he warned against the imposition of any social and political agenda on the university that might jeopardize its academic standards. He was against the rationing of seats among castes and communities, and said, 'Education should not be used for creating or deepening the very inequalities it is designed to prevent' (Government of India 1950: 52).

There was a genuine desire in the wake of independence to create a university that would be different from one that was primarily an institution for the production of graduates and with examination and the award of degrees as its primary concerns. Many of the leaders in the fields of science and scholarship had been exposed to the best universities in the West and been inspired by their achievements. The type of university that served as the inspiration for many has been called the 'Humboldtian university' (Shils 1997: 234–49) after Wilhelm von Humboldt who created its prototype in the University of Berlin in 1810. Humboldt's university first established its presence in Europe, and especially Germany, and then extended its influence into the United States. It had its greatest influence from the middle of the nineteenth to the middle of the twentieth century when the era of the mass university began.

This type of university which prevailed at Berlin, Jena, Heidelberg, Cambridge, Oxford, Harvard, Princeton, Chicago, and elsewhere was a small and compact community of scientists and scholars. It was an open and secular institution, or at least became increasingly open and secular with the passage from the nineteenth to the twentieth century. It sought to embody the unity of teaching and research, and to cover within its scope all principal disciplines from physics to philosophy. It also sought to embody the principle of self-governance and to insulate itself from interference by church and state. It was very different in character and composition from the mass universities that gained increasing ground after World War II and decolonization (ibid.: 3–128).

* * *

Some have begun to wonder if the Humboldtian university can survive even in the United States where it had attained its greatest success by the middle of the twentieth century (Shils 1997). What I would like to discuss here is the prospect of that kind of university in India in the twenty-first century. The problems that face the Indian university today are many and diverse, and yet there are those who speak and write about them as if they believe that we might, by some feat of ingenuity, be able to create here the kind of university that enjoyed such great success in the Western countries for more than a hundred years (Chapter 11).

Our own older universities, the ones that were set up before independence—Calcutta, Bombay, Madras, Delhi, Agra, Mysore, and so on—have expanded enormously in size. Many of the new ones are also very large. Today, they count their members not in the thousands but in the hundreds of thousand.

The Humboldtian university, designed to be a community of scholars and scientists committed to the unity of teaching and research, was very small in size. Right until World War II, such universities as Cambridge, Oxford, Harvard, Princeton, and Chicago had a membership of only a few thousand. Even today, when the size of such a university approaches 20,000, its reflective members begin to worry if it is not becoming a 'mass university'. As a sociologist, I am only too well aware that a radical change in the size of an institution leads inevitably to changes in its form and functioning. In what follows I will discuss mainly the older type of universities which seek to cover all branches of knowledge as against some of the newer ones with a more specific focus, as on law, agriculture, or education. Personally speaking, when I think of the Indian university, my mind turns inevitably to the University of Calcutta where I was a student or the University of Delhi where I have taught for many years.

As I have pointed out, the typical Indian university has expanded enormously in size and scale of operation in the last half century. It is difficult to see how the all-purpose university, with its mandate to cover every subject, can be restrained in its drive for expansion. At the same time, the more it expands, the further it departs from the ideal of the university as a community of scholars and scientists.

In the nineteenth century it did not appear unrealistic for the university to seek to accommodate all the principal disciplines even when each of them remained relatively small in size. The number of disciplines considered suitable for adoption by the university was itself small. This has changed drastically in course of time. Well into the twentieth century, the universities remained highly selective in adopting new subjects and courses of study. Some instruction, mainly of a technical nature, was provided outside the university, and some research too was done outside it. It was through a strict definition of what constituted an academic discipline that the universities were able to remain small and yet sustain the belief that they were responsible for the cultivation of all significant branches of learning.

The last 200 years have witnessed an enormous growth in systematic knowledge. The universities have contributed substantially to this growth, but it will be a mistake to believe that they alone have contributed to it. In the nineteenth century, many of the pioneers of what were to be adopted later by the universities as branches of social science worked outside them. David Ricardo, John Stuart Mill, Walter Bagehot, Herbert Spencer, and E.B. Tylor, all worked outside the universities to lay the foundations of what are now taught as academic subjects in the universities. It is true that Karl Marx had a first-rate education in the best universities, but he did all his creative work outside them.

The expansion of knowledge has been accompanied by differentiation and specialization. The universities played a major part in this. They defined the boundaries of disciplines, and served to separate one discipline from another by organizing them into departments and faculties. But they were not alone in doing so. The emerging professional associations also contributed to the differentiation and specialization of disciplines.

Before academic specialization had attained its present scale, it was possible for scholars, whether within or outside the universities, to interact fruitfully and meaningfully across a variety of fields. The same scholar published treatises on what would now be regarded as quite different academic disciplines. Herbert Spencer, the most renowned British sociologist in the nineteenth century, published books on a great variety of subjects. He began with *Principles of Statics*, and subsequently published *Principles of Biology*, *Principles of Psychology*, and, then, *Principles of Sociology*. He did not hold any university position but worked for some time as sub-editor for *The Economist*, of which Walter Bagehot, the author of a renowned work on the English constitution, was the editor.

Things began to change as the division of labour between disciplines became more and more elaborate in the twentieth century. The universities themselves played an important part in this by organizing and reorganizing disciplines into departments, faculties, schools, and centres. Much of the impulse for the creation and adoption of new disciplines came from ambitious and energetic deans and heads who sought to expand and consolidate their own spheres of influence. Today the disciplines and fields of study and research recognized by the universities and accommodated in them number in the scores. At least in India, the resolve to promote interdisciplinary study and research has had little effect in creating active lines of communication among the increasing number of disciplines and branches of study. The idea that the multi-purpose university covering all branches of study from physics to philosophy via computer science, gender studies, and peace studies can function as a single community of scholars and scientists has become increasingly remote from the reality.

There are other reasons why the universities have expanded their scale of operation. In India the most important among these is the urge to make them socially more inclusive through the accommodation of all classes and communities, and all sections of society. The socially inclusive university is an idea of the twentieth century, and more particularly of the second half of it. It was only after World War II and decolonization that the universities came under increasing pressure to become socially more inclusive and began to expand their scale of operation in response to that pressure (Chapter 11).

* * *

The universities have expanded their size and scale of operation, and they have acquired many new functions in the course of their expansion. It is in this context that we must ask whether each single university can adequately perform all the tasks of teaching, research, and examination in the entire range of recognized disciplines that it is expected to perform. My view is that the university of the twenty-first century must limit its scale of operation and, hence, its ambition to be a 'universal' site for the creation and transmission of systematic knowledge.

I have heard many high-minded scholars and scientists, including some of my own colleagues, say that our universities have sunk to the status of factories for the production of BAs, MAs, and PhDs without any serious concern for standards of teaching and research. But our first universities were set up in 1857 not for undertaking teaching and research but for conducting examinations and awarding degrees. Hence, if that is now the major concern of so many of our universities, it is not a deviation from the original purpose of the Indian university, but a return to it.

The university cannot disown its responsibility to produce graduates, but it must at least try to ensure that it is not overwhelmed by that one single responsibility. Producing employable graduates is an important responsibility of the university, but it is not its sole responsibility and not, in every case, even its main responsibility.

There are many reasons why the pressure on the universities to produce more graduates will not decrease in the foreseeable future, but increase. India has an expanding middle class whose expansion will not brook any restraint. As the ranks of the salaried middle class expand, the need for more graduates will also expand. The universities at Calcutta, Bombay, and Madras, unlike those at Cambridge, Oxford, and Paris, were set up to nurture the growth of an educated middle class, and it is difficult to see how they can renege on this responsibility when that class is acquiring increasing importance, not only politically and culturally but also demographically.

University degrees cannot eliminate social inequality, but they are an important aid to individual mobility. What social and political commentators usually mean when they say that they want inequality to be ended is that they want the obstacles to individual mobility to be removed or relaxed. The universities may not have brought inequality to an end, but they have acted as important catalysts for individual mobility. This may not be the same thing as the advancement of science and scholarship, but it is nevertheless an important social function in a democracy.

Nobody can deny that the universities have contributed something to individual mobility, first by enabling individuals to move into the middle class as clerks and other lower-grade non-manual employees, and then by enabling their offspring to move upward in that class as lawyers, doctors, and civil servants. Many feel, however, that they have not contributed enough to this process and should be required to contribute more. How much more they can contribute to individual mobility and through what procedures is not a subject that I can discuss on this occasion. But one thing should be clear: we cannot force the pace of individual mobility through university education too far or for too long without compromising the academic standards of the university.

In a country that is as large and as diverse as ours, we must look at the university system as a whole. In our circumstances today it is not necessary for each and every university to undertake all the major activities that must come under the care of the university system of a nation. Not all universities can be expected to give the same attention to undergraduate and postgraduate teaching, or to teaching and research. But whatever it might do, no university in the twenty-first century can be exempted from the responsibility of conducting examinations and awarding degrees. At the same time, that responsibility will remain a serious, not to say an unbearable, burden if each university has to conduct examinations for hundreds of thousands of students every year.

The universities of the twenty-first century cannot be set up with the same objectives with which our first universities were set up in 1857; nor, when set up, should they be encouraged to follow the same trajectories that the earlier ones did. We have accepted the principle that a university today does not have to be universal in its coverage of disciplines in order to engage in the combined pursuit of teaching and research at the highest level of excellence.

If the new universities seek to be all-encompassing like the old ones, they are not likely to meet with much success in the twenty-first century. Universities, like many other public institutions in India, have a natural tendency to expand. Many of them have in the recent past been willing to undertake whatever was required of them, provided funds were made available. Universities can be effective as centres of advanced study and research only if they exercise restraint in what they undertake to do. They must not expand recklessly even if this means a limitation on the funds they are able to secure and on the powers that their vice-chancellors can exercise.

An institution will scarcely deserve to be called a university if it undertakes only teaching and no research, or only research and no teaching. And it will not deserve that name if it is devoted exclusively to only one single discipline. There is no reason to move from an extremely wide to an unduly narrow band of subjects. The viable university that I have in mind will have a cluster of disciplines with, perhaps, a core and a periphery. Not all universities need to have the same core or the same periphery.

The kind of university that had its greatest success in the second and third quarters of the twentieth century had at its core the arts and sciences, comprising disciplines such as philosophy, history, languages, mathematics, physics, and chemistry, with professional subjects such as law and medicine at the periphery (Parsons and Platt 1973). Harvard is an outstanding example. That kind of university will and should continue to exist in the future. But there will be other types as well, with science and technology, or economics and management, or law, or education at the core. The cluster has to be carefully selected and organized; it cannot be some ad hoc arrangement put together from existing institutions that are themselves declining or moribund. Again, such an institution can prosper in the future only if its reckless expansion is prevented.

References

Government of India. 1950. *The Report of the University Education Commission, 1948–49*. New Delhi: Ministry of Education.

Nehru, Jawaharlal. 1958. *Speeches: 1946–49*, vol. 1. New Delhi: Government of India.

Parsons, Talcott and Gerald M. Platt. 1973. *The American University*. Cambridge, Massachusetts: Harvard University Press.

Shils, Edward. 1997. *The Calling of Education*. Chicago: University of Chicago Press.

Index